Reclaim Your Sovereignty
Take Back Your Christian Name

Copyright © 2009
by
David E. Robinson

MAINE-PATRIOT.com
3 Linnell Circle
Brunswick, Maine 04011

maine-patriot.com

Reclaim Your Sovereignty

RECLAIM YOUR SOVEREIGNTY
Take Back Your Christian Name

Contents

Reclaim Your Sovereignty

"Good name in man or woman, dear my lord,
Is the immediate jewel of the soul:
Who steals my purse, steals trash;
'tis something, nothing; 'Twas mine, 'tis his,
and has been slave to thousands;
But he that filches from me my good name
Robs me of that which not enriches him,
and makes me poor indeed."

Othello, the Moor of Venice,
Act III, Scene 3,
by William Shakespeare.

Reclaim Your Sovereignty

"Christ in you, the hope of glory."
— *Colossians 1:27.*

Reclaim Your Sovereignty

"Neither slavery nor involuntary servitude ... shall exist within the United States, or any place subject to their jurisdiction."

— *Article 13 of the Bill of Rights*

Reclaim Your Sovereignty

Introduction

What is "the red pill"?

"The red pill" is a term used in the movie *The Matrix,* to refer to "the undistorted truth."

What distorts truth? False belief.

Consider this:

The phrase "I don't believe it" implies that something is evident but that one does not or will not accept it because the evidence does not fit an existing belief (i.e. an existing denial).

"I don't believe it" is often the first thing someone says when he eventually accepts that which becomes obvious to him in due time.

This information is presented not just to dissolve mistaken belief, but to provide information that may not be readily available to a person who is unaware.

The phrase "There is no such thing as..." is the epitome of superstition or denial. Disillusionment is the dissolution of an illusion and a return to wonder, to innocence, and to truth.

Welcome to the information presented herein.

1
Look Behind The Veil

"The one aim of these financiers is world control by the creation of inextinguishable debts." — Henry Ford.

Since 1933 all *other* Americans, except the financiers, have been pledged for the debt of the UNITED STATES owed to international bankers who are mostly foreign to America. Your credit, labor, property and produce are being used as collateral, without your knowledge or consent, by the corporate UNITED STATES. This is legal until you rescind your *implied consent* by an administrative process of law.

You have unknowingly *volunteered* to be chattel for a mortgage held by the financiers from the founding of this nation. You think that the name on the tax statements and bills that you receive is yours, so you respond as though it is, in . . .

voluntary servitude.

To make this servitude legal, it was necessary for the government to *"leave a hole in the fence"* so to speak. It doesn't matter if the escape route is hidden by legal words of art to make escape difficult. That the escape route is not used *presumes your consent*. Escape is *possible* but seemingly *difficult* and even *implausible.*

Your subjection to this *democracy* is based upon the *presumption* that if you did not wish to be so enslaved you would utilize the law to do something about it. As long as you do not take advantage of the escape route provided by law, it is *presumed* that you are content to be in the *pasture* and used as *chattel*. *Chattel* has the same root as *cattle*. Get the picture?

Can such a premise be true?

This seems to be contrary to everything we have ever known about our world, our nation, and our relationship to mankind.

Our parents never behaved as though they we were chattel, did they? They dutifully paid their taxes, voted in elections, and waved the American flag on the 4th of July.

Our teachers taught us about our history, our Declaration of Independence and the Constitution of our Republic, about our Revolutionary War, how we fought the greatest army and navy that the world had ever seen at that time. Nowhere in our history classes did we encounter any such premise of subjection to the central government that rules over our lives today. Our Civics teachers never told us anything about this.

Nothing in our world even hinted that we are the servants of a highly centralized government. This might be true of *other* people in *other* lands, but not of us here in America . . . For most intelligent Americans this cannot possibly be true.

The truth *cannot be heard* because it is so much in discord with our entire worldly experience.

Do not take the expression *"cannot be heard"* as just a figure of speech. In practical conversation this turns out to be true. Either a person will miss what is being said entirely, or if he hears it at all, he will argue — fight the concept — refuse to accept it.

If you are an *exception,* count yourself *open* and blessed. You have in your grasp right now knowledge that can help you escape.

We know now that George Washington did not chop down a cherry tree; that Lincoln did not free the slaves (they became subjects of the federal District of Columbia instead); that General Zachary Taylor provoked the War with Mexico, along the Nueces River; that the battleship Maine was blown up from the inside; that Woodrow Wilson knew that the Lusitania was carrying US munitions to the war in Europe and would be sunk; that Franklin Delano Roosevelt maneuvered the Japanese into an attack on Pearl Harbor and cut off fuel shipments to the Pacific fleet to ensure the presence of enough old ships to offer a tempting target to the Japanese; that Harry Truman knew that there were other good alternatives to an invasion of Japan and that he did not need to drop the Atomic Bomb on Hiroshima and Nagasaki; that Roosevelt knew about the NAZI concentration camps; that LBJ knew that there was no attack on the Maddox and Turner Joy in the Gulf of Tonkin when he asked for a Congressional Resolution to attack North Vietnam; and that the US government had been warned by numerous documented sources that there would be an attack on the Twin Towers of the World Trade Center in New York, and on the Pentagon in Washinton, D.C. All of this is from documented historical sources, yet we continue to believe the myths in our history books, our movies, our mainstream media, and our mass beliefs.

President John F Kennedy warned us:

"The great enemy of the truth is very often not the lie — deliberate, contrived and dishonest — but the myth — persistent, persuasive and seemingly real."

You may find it hard to believe that we have been living in an illusion for our whole lives.

Much of what we believe is an illusion, and we will only find our freedom when we can allow ourselves to look behind the veil, and see Reality.

2
Conspiracy To Defraud

Who you are is far greater than What you perceive yourself to be.

When you have the courage to face the illusion and call it what it is, you will have accomplished the most difficult task before you today. *There IS a way out!*

We have been told the truth repeatedly, but we have not heard. We have the opportunity to take back our sovereignty.

The Conspiracy to Defraud is best explained in the comments of one of the major instigators of the non-federal Federal Reserve. "Colonel" Edward Mandell House is alleged to have said the following to President Woodrow Wilson in 1912:

"Very soon, every American will be required to register his *biological property* [*his body*] in a national system designed to keep track of the people that will operate under the ancient system of *the pledge.* By such methodology, we can compel people to submit to our agenda, which will effect *our security[1]* as a *charge-back[2]* for our fiat paper currency. Every American will be forced to *register[3]* or suffer being unable to work and earn a living. They will be our *chattel,* and we will hold the *security interest[4]* over them forever, by operation of the *law merchant[5]* under the scheme of secured transactions. Americans, by unknowingly or unwittingly delivering the *bills of lading[6]* to us, will be rendered insolvent and bankrupt, forever to remain economic slaves through taxation secured by their pledges. They will be stripped of their rights and given a **commercial value[7]** designed to make us a profit and they will be none the wiser, for not one man in a million could ever figure out our plans and, if by accident one or two should figure it out, we have in our arsenal *plausible deniability.* After all, this is the only logical way *to fund government,* by floating liens and debt to *the* **registrants[8]** in the form of *benefits and privileges.* This will inevitably reap to us huge profits beyond our wildest expectations and leave every American a contributor to this fraud which we will call **social insurance[9]**. Without realizing it, every American will insure us for any loss we may incur and in this manner every American will unknowingly be our servant, however begrudgingly. The people will become helpless and without any hope for their *redemption* and we will employ the high office of the President of our **dummy corporation[10]** to foment this plot against America."

Footnotes to the above:

[1] **Security:** such as when a mortgage company has a security interest in your home.

[2] **Chargeback:** = credit, in bookkeeping language, as when you return something you have bought with your credit — the purchase is *charged back* onto the account. The credit, in this case, is the interest paid by the US Treasury on behalf of the public to the Federal Reserve for the Fed's congress bestowed right to print money, that the US Treasury could print

itself. This massive scam has been in place since the creation of the Federal Reserve Bank, in 1913.

[3] **Register:** for Social Security benefits.

[4] **Security interest:** again refers to "security" as when a mortgage company has *a security interest* in your home.

[5] **Law merchant:** international merchant law is the Uniform Commercial Code (UCC).

[6] **Bills of lading:** registration forms, certificates of Live Birth, now used as collateral for the debt of the DISTRICT UNITED STATES.

[7] **Commercial value:** the value assigned to the registration forms, certificates of Live Birth, as collateral for the national debt. This is the nominal value of the life of a human being, considered now, to be 1,000,000 dollars each.

[8] **Registrants:** those registered in the Social Security "Mark of the Beast."

[9] **Social insurance:** now called Social Security.

[10] **Dummy corporation:** THE UNITED STATES (ALL CAPS) is an British corporation under the UCC, not the united States of America united under the Constitution.

We know now how to respond to this treasonous fraud.

All my life I've looked for the roots of injustice, oppression and war because, if we can uncover the basis of the rampant injustice in the world, we might relieve enormous struggles and suffering.

I've wondered about how little the Constitution affects the courts today, and how often the truth is buried in silence.

I see the greed and heartlessness of a power struggle played out in politics today. But it never occurred to me that a game was being secretly played throughout history. Ultimately, it's a game of fiscal policy and politics, with a spiritual bent.

Like many, I've participated for many years in the mythical American scene.

I've written letters to editors, congressmen, senators, presidents; distributed campaign literature to precincts; represented my precinct at conventions; served food at welfare halls; confronted police threatening to arrest people who had taken over HUD homes designed for the homeless; worked with Welfare Moms; supported church social ministries; fasted; spoken to churches on social justice; supported the protestors of demonstrations against the manufacture of cluster bombs; been persecuted for a "wartoy" protest; and marched in protest of the Vietnam War; the Gulf War; and the attacks on Serbia and Kosovo, and now Iraq and other countries in the Middle East.

Yet unable to fathom the truth.

3
Sovereignty, Revolution & A New Nation's Birth

Yes. Our forefathers fought one of the bloodiest wars in world history and won their independence. They understood the historical roots of war, injustice and oppression, and *we've lost this knowledge.* Our history books did, indeed, leave out a lot of the truth and lied about much of the rest. History teachers often teach history in such a way that young students swear to never study history again.

We have been led and lulled to forget WHO WE ARE. This has been engineered by those who would keep us ignorant of the truth.

The primary reason for the American War for Independence was not "taxation without representation" but the forced payment of taxes to the King of England in gold instead of in paper money. America was flourishing by using her own fiat money system *based on production* instead of a gold-based system that could be manipulated by the King.

The King could not *control* the fiat money system and therefore passed a law requiring that taxes to the King be paid only in gold. The King had most of the gold and the colonists had little. Unemployment in the colonies ensued, and the embittered colonists cried out for war.

Benjamin Franklin put it this way:

"The colonies would have gladly born the little tax on tea, and other matters, had it not been that England took away from the colonies their money."

Prior to the Revolutionary War, *The Times of London* said this regarding fiat money in America:

"If this mischievous financial policy, which has its origins in North America, shall become endurrated down to a fixture, then that government will furnish its own money without cost. It will pay off debts and be without debt. It will have all the money necessary to carry on its commerce. It will become prosperous without precedent in the history of the world. The brains and the wealth of all the countries will go to North America. That country must be destroyed or it will destroy every Monarchy on the globe."

The truth is that the American Revolution failed!
You might say that we won a military victory over the most powerful military force on the planet at the time. However, in reading the Treaty of Paris it is clear that we were not negotiating this treaty as victors.

We had won the recall of British troops, but not the recall of the bankers!

Even though we are taught that we won our independence from England, we were only able to remain free from the international bankers for a few years.

The most visible of the power structure was the East India Company owned by the bankers and the Crown in London, England. This was an entirely private enterprise whose flag was authorized by Queen Elizabeth in 1600 — thirteen red and white horizontal stripes with a blue rectangle in its upper left-hand corner.

All debts owed before the war were to be collected by the foreign creditors.

When the creditors of the new nation found the Articles of Confederation to be inadequate to exact payment from their young debtor, the Constitution was written by the bankers, and supported through their associates, to increase their control over the United States of America.

Had the Articles of Confederation been completed and adopted, instead of the devised Constitution, the bankers would have had far less control.

Any constitution must have some prior reference to establish its foundation. The authority for the American Constitution is based upon the **Bible**; the **Magna Carta**, signed in 1215 by King John; the **Petition of Rights**, granted by King Charles I in 1628; the **English Bill of Rights**, granted by William and Mary in 1689; the right of **Habeas Corpus**, granted by King Charles II, and the **Articles of Confederation**. *Any and every constitution thereafter must have an enabling clause.* From this point onward, no constitution may diminish, in any manner, those rights already established in the above **six documents**.

The Declaration of Independence established that the people are sovereign under God's Natural Law. *Sovereign people of the various states created the state governments for the protection of their rights.* They delegated certain authority from the people's powers by and through the state constitutions in order that the three branches of government could properly carry out the dictates outlined in the State constitutions to protect our rights.

In the Declaration of Independence the word "united" in

the phrase "thirteen **united States of America**" is in lower case, whereas in the Constitution it is **United States** (Upper/lower case) — without the qualifying words "of America." Nowhere in these documents is it UNITED STATES (ALL CAPS), or UNITED STATES OF AMERICA (ALL CAPS).

The (ALL CAPS) UNITED STATES OF AMERICA refers to a corporation incorporated in England, not a country.

The Constitution of the American Republic created a new structure of government that was established on a much higher plane than either the *parliamentary system* or the *confederation of states.* It was a people's *"constitutional republic,"* wherein a certain amount of power was delegated to the states and a limited lesser amount of power was delegated to the federal government.

The united States, by way of the Congress of the united States, has certain powers delegated to it by the Constitution. So far as the several States that are party to the Constitution are concerned, the united States may not exercise power not delegated to it by the Constitution. All power not delegated to the united States of America by the Constitution is reserved to the several States within their respective territorial borders — or, to the People.

4

British Subversion, Banks & Treason

Although the Treaty of Paris ended the Revolutionary War in 1783, the simple fact of our existence threatened the monarchies where it hurt most . . . financially.

The United States stood as a heroic role model for other nations, which inspired them to also struggle against oppressive monarchies. The French Revolution (1789-1799) and the Polish uprising (1794) were in part encouraged by the American Revolution.

Although we stood like a *beacon of hope* for most of the world, *the monarchies regarded the United States as a political infection,* the principle source of the radical democracy that was destroying monarchies around the world. The monarchies realized that if the principle source of that infection could be destroyed the rest of the world might avoid the *contagion,* and the monarchies would be saved.

Knowing they couldn't destroy us militarily, they resorted to the more covert methods of political and financial subversion, employing spies and secret agents skilled in bribery and legal deception; it was perhaps the first "cold war" to be waged. In the Jay Treaty (1794) the United States agreed to pay £600,000 lbs. sterling to King George III, *as reparations for waging the American Revolutionary War.*

The US Senate ratified the treaty in secret session, and ordered that it not be published.

When Benjamin Franklin's grandson published it anyway (*perhaps our first whistleblower*) the exposure and resulting public up-roar so angered the Congress that it passed the Alien and Sedition Acts (1798) so federal judges could prosecute editors and publishers for reporting the truth about the government.

Since we had supposedly won the Revolutionary War, *why would our Senators agree to pay reparations to the supposed loser of the war?* And why would our Senators agree to pay £600,000 lbs. sterling *eleven years after the war ended?* It doesn't make sense, especially in light of the Senate's secrecy and later fury over being exposed… *unless our Senators had been bribed to serve the British monarchy and betray the American people.*

This is treason!

5
Bank Fraud, Bribery & Corruption

Chief among the international financiers was Amshel Bauer of Germany who, in 1748 opened a goldsmith shop under the name of Red Shield. (*In German the name is spelled Rothschild and is pronounced Rote-shilld*).

In 1787, Amshel (Bauer) Rothschild made the famous statement: *"Let me issue and control a nation's money, and I care not who writes the laws."* He had five Sons *Amshel Mayer, Solomon, Jacob, Nathan,* and *Carl.* In 1798, the five Rothschild brothers expanded by opening banks in *Germany, Vienna, Paris, London,* and *Naples.*

The objective behind these banks was *to gain the special privilege to use fractional reserve banking to print and loan money to the government and industry. No money could go into circulation without interest being paid to the bankers for its use.*

Fractional reserve banking is quite simple.

It is simply *a special privilege* that is given to a group of men *to create credit out of thin air* and loan this *credit-debt* to anyone else in society. Then, by collecting the money back from society, *plus interest,* they become very rich from what they simply create out of nothing.

The basic mathematics behind this system is very clear.

If this system is left in place long enough, the man or the group who controls this *system of debt creation* will own all the gold available in the nation. Once the supply of real money (gold) is in their hands, *this group of men becomes the controlling master (Dictator)of the entire nation.*

Why?

Because this group of men control the only source of operating medium (*money*) available through which the nation functions. Only the men who have been given the *privilege of printing money and loaning money at interest* can determine who gets special funding — their allies and friends.

Everyone else is limited to how much money they have access to. Therefore, after two or three generations, the allies and friends of these "bankers" will own everything in the nation — *as The United States is now owned by a small cadre of very wealthy men.*

How long this process takes to work its way through the wealth of a nation depends upon how successful the "bankers" are in forcing (*through bribery and corruption*) the formal government's restriction on issuing its money.

As the supply of money shrinks, the people of the nation are forced to rely on the *creation of a fictitious debt* by the privileged few, to a greater and greater extent, until finally, the only thing left is a massive amount of "unpayable debt" created from nothing and consisting only of the *interest* charged upon the fictitious debt, accruing interest for every moment of its existence. All for the benefit of the privileged few who become *the illegally usurping government,* because of the "money power" that they wield.

Through the Bank of England, the Rothschilds demanded a private bank in the United States to hold the securities of the United States as the pledged assets to the Crown of England in order to secure the debt to which our government is in default.

As one of his first official acts, *President Washington declared a financial emergency.* William Morris, with the help of Alexander Hamilton, Secretary of Treasury, heavily promoted the creation of a *private bank* to service the debt to the international bankers in Europe.

Congress chartered the first national bank in 1791 for a term of 20 years to hold the securities of the same European bankers who had been holding the debts *before the Revolutionary war.*

The bankers loaned *worthless, un-backed, non-secured paper money* to each other to charter this first bank, and on December 12, 1791, the first, private, Bank of the United States opened its doors in Philadelphia.

Under public international law, Great Britain (*the creditor nation*), forced the United States to establish a private bank in America to hold the securities as the collateral for the United States national debt to the Crown.

James Madison had warned:

> **"History records that the money changers have used every form of abuse, intrigue, deceit, and violent means possible to maintain their control over governments by controlling money and its issuance."**

Reclaim Your Sovereignty

6
The United States Bank

From the beginning, the Bank of the United States had been opposed by the Democratic Republicans led by Thomas Jefferson, but the Federalists (*the pro-monarchy party*) won the vote permitting the bank's establishment.

The initial capitalization was $10,000,000, *80% of which this capitalization would be owned by foreign bankers.* Since the bank was authorized to lend up to $20,000,000 (*double its paid capital*), it was a profitable deal for both government and the bankers, since the *bankers* could lend and collect interest on $10,000,000 of the banker's assets that didn't even exist.

The European bankers outfoxed the U.S. government. By 1796 the U.S. government owed $6,200,000 in loans to the bank and was forced to surrender most of its shares to the bankers. After 1802 the U.S. government owned no stock in the United States Bank.

Thomas Jefferson had warned,

"If the American people ever allow private banks to control the issuance of their currency, the banks will, first by inflation then by deflation, deprive the people of all property until their children wake-up homeless on the continent their fathers conquered. The issuing power should be taken from the banks and restored to the people, to whom it properly belongs."

Several short-lived attempts to impose the central banking scheme on the United States were defeated by the patriotic efforts of Presidents Madison, Jefferson, Jackson, Van Buren and Lincoln.

7
British Subversion, Titles of Nobility & Treason

During the early decades of U.S. history, relations between the United States and Great Britain remained strained. Their relationship deteriorated sharply with the outbreak of War in Europe in 1803. Britain imposed a blockade on neutral countries such as the United States. In addition, the British impressed (seized) American sailors from their ships and forced them to serve in the British Navy.

Concerned about the many English spies and troublemakers, Congress passed a 13th Amendment to the Constitution to prevent anyone who had an English title, and connections with England, from obtaining any seat in government of the United States; called the Titles of Nobility Act (TONA), it reads as follows:

"If any citizen of the United States shall accept, claim, receive, or retain any title of nobility or honour, or shall without the consent of Congress, accept and retain any present, pension, office, or emolument of any kind whatever, from any emperor, king, prince, or foreign power, *such person shall cease to be a citizen of the United States, and shall be incapable of holding any office of trust or profit under them, or either of them.*"

Titles of nobility had been prohibited in both Article VI of the Articles of Confederation (1777) and in Article I, Section 9 of the Constitution for the United States (1787), *but there was no penalty for breach of this Act.* A title of nobility amendment was deemed necessary, and was proposed in 1789, and again in 1810, and finally approved, passed and ratified in 1819. But the notice of ratification — *which was delivered to the Secretary of State, an attorney with the title of nobility: Esquire* — disappeared. As a result, *there is still no penalty for accepting titles or emoluments from foreign rulers today, just the prohibition against it.*

Clearly, the founding fathers saw such a serious threat in *titles of nobility* and *honours* that anyone receiving such would be required to forfeit his citizenship.

Obviously this original 13th Amendment carried much more significance for our founding fathers than is readily apparent today. *They* knew *that our freedom could be subverted from inside our government and had sought to prevent such a bitter betrayal.*

Today most Senators and Congressmen, all Federal judges, and many of our Presidents are attorneys who carry the title "Esquire," often abbreviated as "Esq." The Constitution still forbids this, nevertheless *without penalty.*

In Colonial America, attorneys trained attorneys, but most held no *title of nobility nor of honor. There was no requirement that a person be a lawyer* to hold the position of *district attorney, attorney general,* or *judge;* a citizen's "counsel of choice" was not restricted to being a lawyer, and there were no state or national bar associations. The only organization that certified lawyers was the International Bar Association (IBA), chartered by the King of England, headquartered in the city of London. Lawyers admitted to the IBA received the rank "Esquire" — a British "title of nobility."

"Esquire" was the principle *title of nobility* which the 13th Amendment sought to prohibit from the United States. Why? Because the loyalty of "Esquire" lawyers was suspect!

Lawyers with an "Esquire" behind their names were *agents of the monarchy* and members of an organization whose principle purpose was political and regarded with the same wariness that some people today reserve for members of the KGB or the CIA.

The archaic definition of "honor" (*as used when the 13th Amendment was ratified*) meant *anyone "obtaining or having an advantage or privilege over another."* A contemporary example of an "honor" granted to only a few Americans is the privilege of being a judge: Lawyers can be judges and exercise the attendant privileges and powers, whereas *non-lawyers* generally cannot. We address the judge as, "Your Honor."

By prohibiting "honors," the missing but now found original 13th amendment prohibited any advantage or privilege that would grant some citizens an unequal opportunity to achieve or exercise political power. Therefore, the second *intent* of the original 13th Amendment was to *insure political equality among all American citizens,* by prohibiting anyone, even government officials, from claiming or exercising a special privilege or power (*an "honor"*) *over other citizens.*

Both "esquire" and "honor" would be key targets of the 13th Amendment even today, because while "titles of nobility" no longer apply now quite as they did back in the early 1800's it is clear that an "esquire" or bar attorney receives far better treatment in and by the courts, as well as by the public at large in general, whereas if you represent *your-*

self (*pro se*) or speak as a freeman (*pro per*), you are treated as though you were rabble and therefore *wards of the court.* Your opinions are of little or no importance in court and you are often treated *similarly* by government officials. Because you are not "esquires," or bar attorneys, *you are considered to be a useless eater, a subject of the government,* a subject "out of control."

The concept of "honor" remains relevant possibly more so today than at any previous time in U.S. history, for they, the "honored," are greatly feared and even revered, even by the esquires who are considered to be below them.

Since the Original 13th Amendment has never been repealed all acts of government since 1819 are technically null and void since most lawmakers, prohibited from participation in government by the Constitution and who should even be stripped of their right to be a US Citizen under TONA, have continued to interject themselves into and run the political process.

When the people discovered that European banking interests owned most of the United States Bank, *they saw the sheer power of the banks* and their ability to influence representative government by economic manipulation and outright bribery. On February 20, 1811, Congress therefore refused to renew the Bank's charter on the grounds that *the Bank was unconstitutional.* This refusal led to the withdrawal of $7,000,000 in *specie* (*money in coin form*) by European investors, which in turn, precipitated an economic recession and the War of 1812. This "War" was punishment for America's refusing to do business on the terms of the International Banking families of the House of Rothschild through the first Bank of the United States.

Congress refused to let the National Bank renew its Charter.

Except for Gen. Andrew Jackson's victory in the Battle of New Orleans, *the War of 1812 produced a string of American military disasters.* The most shocking of these was *the British Army's burning of the Capitol,* the President's house, and other public buildings in Washington on August 24 and 25, 1814. (*Americans had previously burned public buildings in Canada.*)

During the War of 1812 our national archives and many libraries and document repositories were burned and most of the evidence of the TONA disappeared. Nevertheless, *the legislature of Virginia ratified the Act,* and it was subsequently printed in many official publications as the 13th Amendment, even in states which had NOT ratified it, such as Connecticut. But beginning in 1832 it began to disappear from texts, although official state publications continued to publish it as late as 1876.

There are undoubtedly other examples of the monarchy's efforts to subvert or destroy the United States; some are common knowledge, others *remain* to be disclosed to the public.

For example, national archivist David Dodge discovered a book called *2 VA LAW* in the Library of Congress Law Library. According to Dodge, *"This is an un-catalogued book in the rare book section that reveals **a plan to overthrow the Constitutional government by secret agreements engineered by the lawyers of the time**."*

This is one of the reasons why the TONA was ratified by the state of Virginia in the particular manner in which it was, although the alleged "notification" thereof was for a long time thereafter claimed to have been "lost in the mail."

Now, there is no public record that this aforementioned book even exists.

That may sound surprising, but according to the *Gazette* (5/10/91), *"the Library of Congress has 349,402 un-catalogued rare books and 13.9 million un-catalogued rare manuscripts."*

There may be secrets buried in that mass of documents even more astonishing than a missing Constitutional Amendment. Yet this image of documentary disarray appropriately describes our situation today: *We are inundated with information that we have not had the time or interest to sort through. As a result **we have lost** a precious treasure in the chaos and turmoil of daily life — **our sovereignty**.*

One amazing aspect of the War of 1812 was the existence of a *depression during wartime.* War always brings a short-term *prosperity* — except in the case of this war.

To understand this, it is important for you to know that *all depressions and recessions are artificially created through the restriction of our medium of exchange — our money.* This restriction keeps money OUT of circulation. Too few dollars available to facilitate production and distribution of goods means poverty and starvation.

The precariousness of government finance during the War of 1812, and the post war recession, convinced the Republican government under James Madison to re-establish a national bank. Thus the Second Bank of the United States was created, in 1816.

On January 9, 1832 The Second National Bank applied for renewal of its charter 4 years early. This time President Andrew Jackson vetoed the Bank's recharter on the grounds that the Bank was unconstitutional, and he successfully paid off the national debt leaving the U.S. with a surplus of

$5,000. He said, *"If congress has the right under the Constitution to issue paper money, it was given them to use themselves, not to be delegated to individuals or corporations."*

On January 30, 1835, President Andrew Jackson attended a congressional funeral in the Capitol building. As he exited the building, Richard Lawrence, an unemployed house painter, pointed a pistol at Jackson and fired. The percussion cap exploded, but the bullet did not discharge. The enraged Jackson raised his cane to strike his attacker, who fired again. The *second* weapon *also* misfired and the sixty-seven-year-old president escaped assassination at close range. Jackson was convinced that Lawrence was hired by his political enemies, *the Whigs,* to stop his plan to destroy the Bank of the United States.

Andrew Jackson *arguably* violated public international law because he denied the creditor his just lien rights on the debtor. However, *the bankers did not lend value (substance) so they had an unperfected lien.* Therefore the law did not actually apply in this case.

The bankers have had the last laugh on Andrew Jackson *though.* Where is he now? He is on currency issued by the central bank of the UNITED STATES — *by the non-federal FEDERAL RESERVE forced on this country by political wile and deceit.*

Reclaim Your Sovereignty

8
End of the American Republic

In 1861 the Southern States walked out of Congress. This created *sine die* (*"without day"*), a situation in which no date, time, and place was specified for Congress to reconvene to carry on legislative business. *This created a constitutional crisis* that the newly elected president, Abraham Lincoln, had to resolve.

The 1973 Introduction to Senate Report 93-549 (*93rd Congress, 1st Session*) summarizes the situation best:

> **"A majority of the people of the United States have lived all of their lives under *emergency rule*. And in the United States, actions taken by the Government in times of great crises have in important ways — at least from the time of the Civil War — shaped *the present phenomenon of a permanent state of national emergency*."**

When the Southern States walked out of Congress on March 27, 1861, the quorum to conduct business under the Constitution for the united States of America was lost. Thus, the only votes that Congress could lawfully take, under parliamentary law, were those to set the time to reconvene, take a vote to get a quorum, vote to adjourn and set a date, time, and place to reconvene at a later date, but instead, *Congress abandoned the House and Senate without setting a day to reconvene.*

Under the parliamentary law of Congress, when this

happened, Congress became *sine die* (*pronounced see-ne dee-a; literally "without day"*) and thus *when Congress adjourned "sine die," it ceased to exist as a lawful deliberative body, and thus the only lawful, constitutional power that could declare war was no longer lawful, or in session.*

The Southern States also ceased to exist *sine die*, by virtue of their secession from the Union, and some state legislatures in the Northern bloc also adjourned *sine die. Thus all of the states that were parties to the Constitution for the united States of America ceased to exist;* and on April 15, 1861, President Lincoln issued an executive order — Lincoln Executive Proclamation 1 — *therefore the united States have been ruled by the President under executive powers, ever since.*

Eventually, Congress reconvened under the military authority of the Commander-in-Chief of the Armed Forces — *not by the Rules of Order for parliamentary proceedings, or by constitutional Law — thus placing the American people under* Martial Rule, *under the "national emergency" of 1861.*

Thus the Constitution for the united States of America ceased to be the acknowledged law of the land. The President, Congress and the courts took it upon themselves *to remake the Union in a new image* under their totalitarian control, even though there were no constitutional provisions in place that would lawfully grant them the power to place the Union of several States under this new form of control.

President Lincoln knew that his executive orders had no force under constitutional Law, so he commissioned General Orders No. 100 (April 24, 1863) to be *a* special military Code to govern his actions under martial law rule and to justify his seizure of power. *This further extended the laws of the District of Columbia* which supposedly extended the provisions of Article I, Section 8, Clauses 17-18 of the Constitution *beyond the ten square miles boundaries* of Washington, D.C. *into the several states.* General Orders No. 100, also called the *Lieber Instructions* or the *Lieber Code,* extended the laws of war and private international law into the American states, and *BY PRESUMPTION the United States became a military conqueror of the people of the several once independent American states.*

This Martial Rule has been hidden from the people and *has never ended.* Lincoln was assassinated before he could complete his plan to constitutionally *reform* the Southern States and *restore* Congress. Ever since 1861 the united States of America *has been ruled under military law by the Commander of Chief of the military* according to the Executive Orders of the President of the UNITED STATES.

Constitutional law under the original Constitution for the American states is enforced only as a matter of *"keeping the peace"* under the provisions of *the Lieber Code* and *martial law rule.*

This *"peace"* is evidenced in the Preamble of the Expatriation Act of 1868.

Under martial law rule, title of ownership is a mere fiction, since *all property belongs to the military* except for such property as the Commander-in-Chief *may in his benevolence exempt* from seizure and taxation, *upon which he allows the "enemy" to reside.*

In proclaiming this first Trading with the Enemy Act, *by Executive Order,* President Lincoln set in place the means by which the federal government could interact *with Americans who* were not *14th Amendment citizens.* They were technically designated to be *"enemies" of the UNITED STATES.* Can you now see how and why *"we the people" are at odds with our "government"?*

In a message to Congress, December 3, 1861, Abraham Lincoln responded to the banker's argument that the people could not be trusted with their constitutional power — *the political, monetary system of free enterprise our Founding Fathers conceived* — by saying:

> **"No men living are more worthy to be trusted than those who toil up from poverty — none less inclined to take or touch aught which they have not honestly earned. Let them beware of surrendering the political power which they already possess which if surrendered will surely be used to close the door of advancement against such as they and fix new disabilities upon them till all liberty shall be lost."**

In 1865 — *just before the close of the Civil War* — President Lincoln declared his *new monetary policy:*

> **"The Government should create, issue, and circulate all the currency and credit it needs to satisfy the spending power of the Government and the purchasing power of consumers. By the adoption of these principles, the taxpayers will be saved immense sums of interest. Money will cease to be master and become the servant of humanity. The privilege of creating and issuing money is not only the supreme prerogative of government, but it is the government's greatest opportunity."**

Had Lincoln's monetary policy been implemented, it would have ushered in a worldwide economic renewal. Unfortunately Lincoln was assassinated a few weeks after his monetary policy was introduced, because he defied the bankers in proposing to print *interest free money* to pay for the war debt. Thus, the government continues to operate under the authority of private laws dictated by the creditor financiers.

"The borrower is servant to the lender."
— Proverbs 22:7.

President Lincoln was *assassinated* before he could *restore constitutional government* to the states and end his *martial law rule* by executive order, and the 14th Amendment to the Constitution *created a new class of citizen* or "status" for the expanded military jurisdiction.

Congress passed laws in 1871 incorporating the District of Columbia as a private foreign corporation by *the District of Columbia Act* by which all the States in the Union were re-formed as *franchises* or *political subdivisions* of the *Corporation* now called THE UNITED STATES OF AMERICA, *creating a newly formed Union of States under the private rule of the bankers.*

The first attempt by Congress to define *citizenship* was in 1866 with the passage of *the Civil Rights Act* (*Revised Statutes section 1992, 8 United States Code Annotated section 1*). This act provides that:

"All persons born in the United States and not subject to any foreign power are declared to be *citizens of the UNITED STATES.*"

This in turn was followed in 1868 by the adoption of the 14th Amendment — United States Code Annotated Amendment 14, declaring:

"All persons born or naturalized in the United States, *and subject to the jurisdiction thereof,* **are citizens of the UNITED STATES and of the State wherein they reside."**

The only people who were under the jurisdiction of *the private bifurcated government of the ten miles square of Washington, D.C.* were the former slaves, government employees, and people born or natualized within the territories owned by the United States. The former citizens of the South who were now captured, became 14th Amendment citizens as well. The remainder of the people could still invoke the power over government through the original jurisdiction of the republic side of the Constitution.

The *new* 13th Amendment was enacted December 18, 1865. And the 14th Amendment July 28, 1868. It was ratified in the southern states *under the force of military, martial law.* The southern states could only obtain their right to exist by ratifying this forced amendment.

Any contract entered under duress is null and void. But the Constitution was no longer in effect following *sine die* and the proclamation of martial law.

The 14th Amendment brought the *freed slaves* (*whose previous owners were private plantation owners*) under the subjection and control of the ten miles square jurisdiction of Washington, D.C. and it offered government protection to any other people who would volunteer to become its subjects.

The 14th Amendment is a good example of the **give-a-little, take-a-lot strategy** that is often used as sugar coating to a *bitter pill.*

Sovereign Citizens had created a *constitutional Republic* to guarantee them their rights. In contrast, the federal government created a *14th Amendment Democracy* to fortify its power over its citizens. It pretends to be taking citizens under its protection, *but the cost of protection is servitude.* Sovereigns may volunteer to become *subjects;* free men and women to become *vassal slaves.*

The 14th Amendment has always been controversial. Many people over the years have questioned the amount of power it vests in the federal government. *Some have questioned its validity.* On one occasion Judge Ellett of the Utah Supreme Court remarked:

> **"I cannot believe that any court in full possession of its faculties could honestly hold that the amendment was properly approved and adopted."**
> — *State v. Phillips, Pacific Reporter, 2nd Series, Vol. 540, Page 941, 942 (1975).*

Even so. The most important point about this amendment is that although it created a new class of citizen it did not have any effect on sovereign Citizens — *both nationals, and 14th Amendment citizens, exist.*

When the Constitution was adopted the people of the United States were Citizens of the several states for whom and for whose posterity the government was established. Each of them was a citizen of the United States at the adoption of the Constitution and all free persons thereafter born within one of the several states became citizens of their State and of the United States of America by birth.

Both classes of citizen still exist.

It's only a privilege to be a "14th Amendment citizen," but *it's a right* to be a "Soveran."

It's up to you to determine which you now are, and which you really want to be. Remember, you *pay* for a *privilege,* whereas a *right* comes at *no charge.*

This is the *heart* of your Declaration of Independence, today.

9

Two Governments / Two Flags; The Corporate State

Once the smoke settled after the Civil War, *the European bankers took over once again.* In 1871 the loan default again loomed, and bankruptcy was imminent. So the ten square mile District of Columbia was incorporated in England. A loophole had been left in the Constitution by lawyers in league with the international bankers that created *a separate nation by the same name,* that Congress ruled according to Article I, Sect. 8, clauses 17, 18:

"The Congress shall have power: To exercise exclusive legislation in all cases whatsoever, over such district (not exceeding ten square miles) as may, by cession of particular States, and the acceptance of Congress, become the seat of government of the United States, and to exercise like authority over all places purchased by the consent of the legislature of the state in which the same shall be, for the erection of forts, magazines, arsenals, dock yards, and other needful buildings; And To make all laws which shall be necessary and proper for carrying into execution the foregoing powers, and all other powers vested by this constitution in the government of the United States, or in any department or officer thereof."

This District of Columbia United States is *a Legislative Democracy* within *the Constitutional Republic* and is known as the Federal United States. It has exclusive and unlimited rule over its citizenry, the residents of the District of Columbia, and its enclaves and territories (*Guam, Midway Islands, Wake Island, Puerto Rico, etc.*), and anyone who is a citizen naturalized by the 14th Amendment.

The same Congress rules both "United States." The *original* united States is a Republic of fifty States that have the Stars and Stripes *without any gold fringe,* as its flag. The *federal* United States is the democracy under military control which has the Stars and Stripes *with the gold fringe seen in schools, libraries, and district courts,* as its flag.

The abbreviations of the states of the *continental united States* under the jurisdiction of the constitutional Republic are Ala., Alas., Ariz., Ark., Cal., etc., without zip codes. The abbreviations of the states of the *district United States,* under the jurisdiction of the legislative Democracy, are AL, AK, AZ, AR, CA, etc., without any periods, but with ZIP codes, Zone ImProvement codes.

The international bankers and the Congress conjured up this mischief and passed it into law. *But whose law?* Congress broke faith with the People and sold us out in 1871 when they formed a *private corporation* by establishing the District of Columbia as the New Order United States. They used the Constitution and the 14th Amendment as their *by-laws* by taking authority not *under* the Constitution, but *over* the Constitution.

They copyrighted the corporate Constitution and many related names such as THE UNITED STATES, US, THE UNITED STATES OF AMERICA, USA, as their own *trademarks.* This was the final blow to the original Constitution of 1787. Henceforth, the UNITED STATES has been governed by *private corporate law, dictated by the banks* as Receivers of the bankrupt UNITED STATES, under the laws of bankruptcy.

The "Act to Provide a Government for the District of Columbia" — *Section 34 of the 41st Congress of the United States, Session III, Chapter 61 and 62, February 21, 1871* — states that *the UNITED STATES OF AMERICA is a corporation* whose jurisdiction applies only to the ten-mile-square area of land known as the District of Columbia, *and to whatever property is legally titled to the UNITED STATES* by being registered in corporate County, State, and Federal jurisdictions under the *military power* of the UNITED STATES and its creditors.

Under this Act, the Congress of the *Military UNITED STATES* obtained the power *to institute private international law* for application *within the federal District of Columbia United States.* All States of the Union adopted new, *legislatively created conditions* and *codified* their laws under federal mandate. *State 'codes'* were unlawfully adopted despite the states' origins as instruments of sovereign people. Even so. *We the people remained sovereign.*

USC Title 28, 3002(15)(a) basically says that the UNITED STATES is a federal corporation. What was not said in 1871, but was implied, is plainly stated in USC Title 28, 3002(15)(b)&(c) that *all departments of the UNITED STATES CORPORATION are sub-divisions of the corporation.* Title 28 of the UNITED STATES CODE is privately copyrighted, international law.

The UNITED STATES CODE, in its entirety, is privately copyrighted, International Law applicable only in the District of Columbia United States.

This incorporating was first reported by a Gary W. Phillips whose career with the Immigration and Naturalization Service (the INS) began in 1956. Phillips was the Director of the INS at Sea Tac International Airport in Seattle Washington for 20 years, who began challenging the fraudulent income tax in 1985 (*Idaho Observer, March, 2000*).

After nearly 40 years of government service, Phillips was forced to flee this country *to protect his life* after exposing the facts of the illegality of the federal government's *criminal income tax collection scam* — facts that are becoming well known among informed people throughout the United States today.

Where did the Congress find the authority in the original 1787-91 Constitution to reconstitute any part of the united States as a corporation?

The original Constitution was simply set aside to make room for the New World Order corporation. Would this Act benefit the Republic? No. *The corporate bottom line is private profit. The municipal, bottom line was public service, instead.*

To replace our **service** oriented form of government with a **profit** oriented form of government — *without our knowledge or consent* — can only be described as Treason.

A few superficial changes were made to *the original Constitution* and it was no longer the real thing.

Congress did not change *the name* of the Constitution so that they can claim to be still reading from the *original* Constitution. They simply changed its name from the *organic* Constitution **for** the United States of America to the corporate CONSTITUTION **OF** THE UNITED STATES.

Note the name "this Constitution for the United States of America" given to the Constitution in its Preamble, and compare it to the name "The Constitution of the United States" in the title of the same page. They changed the word "for" to "of" and capitalized all the letters that refer to a corporation.

All of a sudden we had *two Constitutions* — the **original** for show and the **doctored** for actual use.

Reclaim Your Sovereignty

10
Corporate Version of the Constitution

The Act of 1871 provided a government for the District of Columbia and created a corporation entitled THE UNITED STATES OF AMERICA whose jurisdiction extends only over corporate entities created by the municipal corporation and operates only in the District of Columbia United States.

Washington, D.C. is the capitol of the District of Columbia — no longer the capitol of the united States of America. All laws passed within the District of Columbia are applicable and enforceable only in the District of Columbia and its possessions.

The States of the Republic are not possessions of the District of Columbia. Puerto Rico, the Virgin Islands and Guam are possessions of the District of Columbia, as well as other property legally titled to the UNITED STATES by counties and states.

The UNITED STATES CODE was devised in the District of Columbia as copyrighted, private International Law and is applicable only in the District. By their own rules of jurisdiction UNITED STATES attorneys have no business prosecuting anyone *outside* of the District of Columbia or Federal territories. *Federal courts have no venue outside of the District of Columbia,* and therefore no lawful jurisdiction *outside* of the District of Columbia and its possessions. *The Congress cannot pass a law that's applicable in the several States of the Republic.*

Since all laws of the District of Columbia are private,

International Law (*including the UNITED STATES CODE and all statutes passed after 1871*) which is enforceable only in the District of Columbia, *then how could they have become the law of the land?*

Because we the people allowed it.

We allowed agents of foreign countries to establish an unlawful corporation that has systematically corrupted every state, county, city, and town in this nation, and the status of most people in the united States.

The only way that a UNITED STATES DISTRICT COURT can have jurisdiction over a sovereign American is if he *voluntarily joins that jurisdiction and fails to publicly declare his sovereign independence.*

This corporation has created dozens of alphabet agencies, the IRS, FBI, DEA, and the BATF, *to name but a few,* which employ *thousands of agents who receive excellent salaries and benefits for betraying their friends and families,* while enforcing the private edicts of the so-called Congress. The men and women of Congress smile, speak softly, and then direct their illegal agencies to *destroy* those who do not fully conform to their wishes, and strike *fear* into hearts of those who do. Kidnapping and conspiracy are involved in every arrest and conviction by federal authorities *outside* of the District of Columbia.

The question now leads to whether our duly elected public officials swear an oath to uphold the Constitution **for** the united States of America, the Republic, within which our rights are protected by a service-oriented government. Or swear an oath to the CONSTITUTION **OF** THE UNITED STATES OF AMERICA, the Democracy within which privileges are bestowed by the profit oriented corporation?

It appears by their actions that *most government em-*

ployees, knowingly or unknowingly, *have sworn an oath to* the corporate, democratic UNITED STATES. It is our duty, *as the People who elected them into office,* to demand accountability from our public officials — who are our servants — and confront them as to where their loyalties lie. Is it with the corrupt, treasonous corporation that is controlled by foreign agents, from within and without, or is it with our constitutional Republic, the united States of America, and her citizens?

An articulate defender of a conservative monetary policy, *President James A. Garfield,* urged the *resumption of specie payments and the payment of government debts.* He said:

"Whoever controls the volume of money in any country is absolute master of all industry and commerce."

In his Inaugural Address in 1881, James Garfield said:

"The chief duty of the National Government in connection with the currency of the country is to coin money and declare its value. Grave doubts have been entertained whether Congress is authorized by the Constitution to make any form of paper money legal tender. The present issue of United States notes has been sustained by the necessities of war; but such paper should depend for its value and currency upon its convenience in use and its prompt redemption in coin at the will of the holder, and not upon its compul-

sory circulation. These notes are not money, but "promises to pay promises to pay." [you can redeem a promise to pay and get a promise to pay in return.] *If the holders demand it, the promise should be kept."*

Garfield was assassinated after only two hundred days in office, he died 80 days after being shot by a lawyer, ostensibly because the lawyer was upset about not receiving an ambassadorial commission to France.

In 1909, default loomed once again. The US government asked the Crown of England for an extension of time. *This extension was granted for another 20 years on several conditions,* one of which was that the federal United States *permit its creditors to establish a new private national bank.*

The bankers moved deeper into our nation in 1913 by establishing the non-federal Federal Reserve Bank and the IRS to collect the interest on the banker loans made to the corporate UNITED STATES. *The 17th Amendment (May 31, 1913) to have the senators elected by the people instead of the states,* was one of the conditions for the 20 year extension of time.

The 16th and 17th Amendments reduced the power of the states further as *THE UNITED STATES adopted the mercantile system of ancient Babylonia.*

With the passage of the Federal Reserve Act in 1913, THE UNITED STATES became firmly ensconced beneath the yoke of servitude that a small number of very rich men have been able to lay upon the people, the yoke of slavery itself. That yoke grows heavier with *ever-compounding interest,* now totaling more than $20 trillion dollars of debt owed by the American people today (*$80,000 per American*).

This vast accumulation of wealth concentrates immense power and despotic domination in the hands of a few central bankers *"who are able to govern credit and its allotment, supplying life-blood to the entire economic body, grasping in their hands the very soul of the economy, so that no one dares to breathe against their will."*

11
The First World War

In 1917 the United States was enticed into the First World War. President Woodrow Wilson had to find a way to persuade the American public to go along with a intervention in another European War. Although pledged by the US Neutrality Act to be neutral in the deadly conflict, Wilson had our Navy shepherd British convoys across the Atlantic. German U-boat commanders refused to take the bait and avoided contact with the US destroyers. To *force* the issue, a US Naval ship was ordered to sail into the midst of a battle between the British and German naval fleets, and was sunk. Wilson had to find a way to persuade the American public to intervene in this newest of European wars.

The Lusitania was a speedy warship refitted by the British as a passenger liner. *The Lusitania was carrying a huge cargo of military equipment and munitions in violation of the US Neutrality Act, unknown to its passengers.* The Germans knew this and tried to warn the passengers by placing advertisements in prominent newspapers in the United States. *The US State Department ordered all of the newspapers to refuse the ad.* One newspaper, *in Des Moines Iowa,* bravely published the information.

To ensure a successful provocation, the Lusitania was ordered to sail at 3/4 speed using only three of its four powerful engines. *The naval escort was ordered away leaving the Lusitania vulnerable as it entered the war zone.* The first torpedo hit the explosive cargo below deck and blew the bottom out of the Lusitania. It sank in only 18 minutes. 126 innocent civilians died. Wilson now had his provocation to rally Americans behind the *War to End All Wars.*

The US participation in WWI so increased the national debt that it became impossible for us to pay it off in 1929. It also enhanced *the War Powers Act* that President Lincoln put in place during his Presidency *by Executive Order.* Lincoln's War Powers Act was revised, in 1917, as *the Trading with the Enemy Act* to define, regulate and penalize those who were trading with the enemy, and who were *then* required to be *licensed by the government* to do business in THE UNITED STATES.

Unknown to the general public, *the Trading with the Enemy Act* was used to define, regulate and penalize *Citizens of the constitutional, United States Republic* who were trading with *the corporate, UNITED STATES Democracy* as their enemy, who were then required to be *licensed to do business in THE District UNITED STATES.*

12
The Great Depression; from Sovereignty to Servitude

We all know what happened in 1929.

The year of the stock market crash and the beginning of The Great Depression. The stock market crash removed billions of dollars from the people to the banks. This *also* removed cash from circulation for the people's use. Those who possessed cash invested it in high interest yielding interest Treasury Bonds that were driven even higher by increased demand.

As a result, even more cash was removed from circulation from the people's use to the point where there was not enough cash left in circulation to buy the goods being produced. Production came to a halt as surplus inventory overwhelmed the market. There were more goods on the market than there was available cash to buy them. Prices plummeted as industries plunged into bankruptcy, throwing millions of people out of work. Foreclosures on homes, factories, businesses and farms rose to the highest level in the history of America. A few dimes were literally salvation to many families now living on the street. Millions of people lost everything they had, except the clothes on their backs.

In 1930 the International Bankers in Europe declared several nations bankrupt, including the United States.

When Franklin Delano Roosevelt took office as President, in 1933, *his first act was to publicly declare a Bank Holiday in the United States.*

On March 5, 1933, as Commander in Chief of the Armed

Forces, Roosevelt commanded all UNITED STATES citizens exchange all their gold for paper Federal Reserve Notes. This Executive Order was passed into law by Congress three months to the day, after the fact, on June 5, 1933.

We the people turned in all our gold at that time.

Why? Were we UNITED STATES citizens subject to the Feds?

No. We were sovereign people at that time. We simply *assumed* that we were required to obey Roosevelt and turn in all our gold. Only those people living in Washington, D.C. and 14th Amendment Citizens were ordered to do so. Sovereign state Citizens were not under the jurisdiction of the DISTRICT OF COLUMBIA UNITED STATES, that was incorporated in 1871, in England as a business.

When we surrendered our gold, we were unknowingly *volunteering* to become citizens of the ten miles square jurisdiction of Washington D.C., and its laws.

When we surrendered our gold, we became 14th Amendment Citizens of THE DISTRICT OF COLUMBIA CORPORATE UNITED STATES.

Our birth certificate, the title of ownership to our body, was registered as a security in the Department of Commerce. This title to our body, our property, and our future labor, was pledged to the International Bankers as security (collateral) for the money owed to them by the bankrupted UNITED STATES.

This was done under the authority of maritime law by and through laws of title.

The American people were not bankrupt. Only the CORPORATE UNITED STATES was bankrupted and in bankruptcy.

But with the US Corporation holding the title to your body and your life, you could then be used as collateral to secure the national debt via your birth certificate, registered by your parents in the Commercial Registry of the UNITED STATES. This commercial administrative act, gave the title to your body to the corporate UNITED STATES via a *constructive trust contract.*

The government then created an artificial *"person"* in your name, *a corporation-of-one,* the fictitious strawman to take your place in the virtual reality of fictional corporations and commercial contract law. Then by an *adhesion contract* the government made you, *the real flesh and blood woman or man,* financially responsible as co-signer for that fictional entity, as a *fiduciary and surety* for that *artificial-entity strawman.*

Your artificial-entity strawman secures the National debt, and through it, you and your strawman became a 14th Amendment Citizen of the for-profit, corporate UNITED STATES.

In other words, they got you to think and act as though you were really that fictional-entity strawman. You agreed to this by your actions and your failure to protest.

A contract offer adheres to you because *you act as though you accept the offer,* and by doing so you are *presumed* to accept the contract as well.

All licenses and all existing contracts are made between THE UNITED STATES or THE STATE OF (*where you live*) and your artificial entity, government created strawman. That fictitious entity binds you to THE UNITED STATES and its sub-corporations, because they made you, the real man or woman, a *fiduciary co-signer who is financially responsible* for that artificial entity strawman, and its actions and debts.

Of course. You *voluntarily* signed and even *requested* all those contracts, didn't you? . . . No?

It looks like your name, even though you never *write your name* in all capital letters as you see it printed on their forms. They want you to disregard the *aberration* as just something they do to be clear and error free.

All of these contracts that you sign carry with them *your unknowing agreement* to obey and uphold the *statutes, rules and regulations* passed by the Congress of the DISTRICT UNITED STATES and THE STATE OF (*where you live*) . . . *and they will be enforced* against *you.*

From that day forward, you could never own property *in allodium* (*all the way, totally*) because the State now has possession of it and holds it all.

In 1964, the State obtained title to all *private* property as well. You only "rent" the home that you think you own, by paying taxes. You have a *certificate of title* to the car you think you own, and you are permitted to drive it in exchange for your *yearly registration rent.* The State owns the true title to your home, your car, and to everything else you thought, or think you own, *including your children.* This is Communism in disguise.

You married the State via your marriage license. You and your children are Wards of the State.

All of this was pledged, *including the fruits of your labor and your body,* to the bankers as security against the National Debt and placed in the possession of the Secretary of State of each State, an *Agent* for the *Trustee* of the

Bankruptcy: *the Secretary of the US Treasury.*

By not knowing the rules of the game you went directly to jail. *You did not pass "GO," and you did not collect $200 in this commercial, "Monopoly," money game.*

Reclaim Your Sovereignty

13
Maritime Admiralty Law

There are two kinds of law on the earth. Civil law, which is the law of the land, and Maritime Admiralty law, which is the law of water.

Maritime Admiralty law is banking law, the law of money, having to do with currency and commerce. Maritime Admiralty law says that, because you arrived from your mother's water, you are a Maritime Admiralty product.

This is why the Ship is sitting in it's Birth, and it's tied to the Dock. Its Captain has to give a Certificate of Manifest to the port authorities, because money is changing hands.

When you were born you had to have a "Birth" Certificate that had to be signed by the Doc because that's where the Ship is tied to the Dock. So the Doc signs your Birth Certificate. Why? Because you came down out of your mother's water. You came down her "birth" canal. You are a Maritime Admiralty product, therefore your Birth Certificate was signed by your mother, and where your mother signed on the Birth Certificate, it does not say "Parent" or "Mother," it says "Informant." Your mother was informing the bank that she has just produced another Product (Security) to be bought and sold.

England, the British Crown, through international banking, owns your physical body, and that's the law. You may think it's funny, but you are a Maritime Admiralty product. Therefore the bank owns your body.

On the back of your Social Security Card will be numbers in red, on the front the numbers are blue or black.

The numbers on the back of a Social Security Card, in red, designate your body. It is the Serial Number of your Stock. If you are wealthy, you are a Preferred Stock. If you are poor, you are a Common Stock.

Your body is bought and sold through the use of your Birth Certificate. And if you could get your original Birth Certificate back, called your Birth Record, you would find that on the back of the Birth Record are listed all the banks around the world.

All over the world banks have used your Birth Record, because you are a certified Stock in a Maritime Admiralty banking scheme, where you make money for banks. Consequently, the corporation and government, and people, who want to control you, create a *second* you, your **strawman,** and that second you that they control, that they created, is named with your name in all capital letters.

Check it out, every time you get a bill, get a law suit, a fine, a ticket, or somebody sends you a bill from the telephone or power company. Check it out on your Driver's License, on your Social Security Card, on your Insurance Cards, or bank account, anything have to do with money and business, your name will always appear in all capital letters, because only all capital letters can be dealt with in commerce, by the government and by the banks.

Anytime you see your a name in upper and lower case letters, that applies to you. They've got no control over you. But if you sign a contract in which your name is in all capital letters, they can now take you to court. As a matter of fact, the Judge sits on the Bench. He rules from the Bench, on the Deck. The word "bench" in Latin is "bank."

So the Judge rules from the Bench on the Deck. Right? Cause he's ruling for the bank. Cause somebody's gotta pay.

It's just a game. The Queen of England wants her cut of American blood. She wants her piece of the action. Somebody's gotta pay the tax. And the money's going to go where? Into a bank. That's right. The Judge rules for the bank.

So consequently, if you are working in Maine making money, you are then referred to as a franchisee.

You're a franchisee of a foreign corporation. You work for the Queen of England, the Crown. Your 'butt' is owned by the Queen of England, the Crown, and a corporation called UNITED STATES, while a man called "Obama" is the President of this British corporation. You want to talk Treason?

You need to wake up and find out how this stuff really works, because once you understand it, you don't need to submit yourself, as an American, to a British commercial Venture called courts. You're an American, you don't *need* to go to court. You only go to court because you *agree* to go to court.

When they send you a subpoena to court, or a summons to court, and they've sent you something, you just look at it and say, "Hey, Jack, that's not me. That's in all capital letters. All capital letters is a Corporation. It's a Corps. It's dead. Do I look like I'm dead, to you? No! I'm an American, Jack. I'm not dead. And besides, I'll go to an *American* System for justice. I don't need a British Grand Lodge Masonic system called Court. This British Grand Lodge Masonic system called Inns of Court comes free, out of England, and it has manipulated, exploited, and lied to the people so that everybody in America thinks he has to go to court.

"Oh! They've sent me something that says I've gotta go to court."

I don't go to anybody's court. I'm an American. I don't need to go to court. That's the difference between being a freeman and a slave.

Adopted from *"You Need To Know This,"*
www.tinyurl.com/5ggzvw

14
Cows in the Pasture or Freedom, Your Hidden Choice

The way out of this is dilemma can be very complex. In fact, its complexity is intentional. *Roosevelt violated the law by placing us into involuntary servitude without our consent.*

Congressman Louis T. McFadden brought formal charges against the Federal Reserve Bank and the Secretary of the Treasury, and was coming dangerously close to calling for impeachment of Franklin D. Roosevelt.

On June 5 at 4:30 pm, three months AFTER his Executive Order of March 5, 1933, the Senate and Representatives of the 73d Congress, 1st Session, approved *HJR 192, "Joint Resolution To Suspend The Gold Standard And Abrogate The Gold Clause, Joint Resolution to assure uniform value to the coins and currencies of the United States,"* which formally declared the bankruptcy of the corporate UNITED STATES.

By Executive Order President Roosevelt declared the people outside the federal territories to be enemies of the UNITED STATES that had been illegally amending the Trading with the Enemy Act of 1861 that had been revised in 1917.

The regulation of Federal Zone Citizens tightened up fyrther when PEOPLE applied for SSNs. The benefits that this silent contract offered were voluntarily applied for when the Social Security Act was signed into law in 1935. *Further contracts were to be entered into and licenses to be applied for* — all voluntary actions on the public's part.

We unknowingly entered into lifelong servitude to the Lord of the Manor, UNCLE SAM in order to receive the benefits of servitude. We *unknowingly* volunteered into the feudal plan.

President Roosevelt called all the governors into Washington D.C. for a governors conference. *This was the beginning of the States' loss of their sovereignty and states' rights.* With the BUCK ACT the States lost their influence over the corporate UNITED STATES in 1944.

Under the BUCK ACT the States became 14th Amendment citizens as well. The BUCK ACT completed the destruction of the corporate States' shield of protection against the government of the UNITED STATES. The corporate States went under the jurisdiction of Washington, D.C. at that time.

On October 28, 1977, Public Law 95-147 declared a National Emergency and quietly repealed HJR 192. The "Joint resolution to assure uniform value to the coins and currencies of the United States" (31 U.S.C. 463), approved June 5, 1933, no longer applies to obligations issued on or after the date of enactment of this section. But *public policy allowing the use of Federal Reserve Notes* (promissory notes) *as money substitutes remained unchanged,* and those operating on the privilege of *limited liability* via the public, credit trust are still bound.

The Uniform Commercial Code was adopted by all States in 1964 and a number of other such laws and Acts were incorporated into use at that time. This made the Uniform Commercial Code (UCC) the Supreme Law of the Land, above the Constitution for the united States of America.

15

Equity-Admiralty Courts Replace Common Law

Under the Constitution, the Republic provides for legal cases in Common Law, in Equity Law and in Maritime Admiralty jurisdictions.

1. **Common Law** is the will of *the majority.* Common Law is the substitution of a *common force* for an individual force. Since an individual cannot lawfully use force against the liberty, property or person of another, the *common force* cannot lawfully be used against the liberty, property or person of another individual or group. *Common Law* allows you to do anything you want to do as long as it doesn't infringe upon the life, liberty or property of another. ***Common Law does not compel performance.***

2. **Equity Law** is the will of *contracts* that must be performed under the civil orders of the court. Any contract you are a party to must be obeyed based on what is fair in the particular situation. The term "equity" denotes the spirit and habit of fairness, justness, and right that would regulate the dealings of men with men. You have no rights beyond what is specified in your contracts. Equity Law involves no criminal aspects. ***Equity Law compels performance.***

3. **Maritime Admiralty Law** is the will of *contracts under a criminal penalty for failure to perform. **Ad-***

miralty Law compels performance, under a penalty for failure to perform.

Today's ordinances, statutes, acts, regulations, orders, precepts, etc. are mistakenly *perceived as law,* but just because something is *called a "law"* doesn't make it a law. There is a specific difference between *"legal"* and *"lawful."* *Anything the government does is generally "legal" but it may not always be "lawful."*

By 1938 the merger of law and equity procedures occurred (i.e., the same court has jurisdiction over common law, equity and admiralty concerns).

THE UNITED STATES is bankrupt and is owned by its Creditors. *The international bankers now own everything* — Congress, the Executives, the courts, the States and *their* executives, *and all the land and the people.*

Everything is mortgaged to the national debt.

We've gone from being sovereigns **over** the government to subjects **under** the government, by using negotiable instruments (*promissory notes*) to discharge our debts *with limited liability . . .* instead of paying our debts *at common law* with silver or gold coin.

The change in our system of law from *public, common law to private, commercial law* was instituted by the Supreme Court of the United States in 1938, in **Erie Railroad vs. Thompkins,** when the procedures of common law were blended with the procedures of equity law.

Supreme Court decisions *prior* to 1938 were based on *public law,* according to the Constitution for the United States. Supreme Court decisions *after* 1938 are based on *public policy,* according to the Uniform Commercial Code.

Public policy concerns *commercial transactions* under

the *Negotiable Instrument's Law* — a branch of *the international Law Merchant* (*merchants law*). This system of law has been *codified into the Uniform Commercial Code* that was made uniform in 1964 throughout the fifty States.

By offering grants of negotiable paper (*Federal Reserve Notes*) to the fifty States of the Union, for education, highways, health, and other purposes, *Congress bound the States into a commercial agreement with the federal, DISTRICT UNITED STATES* — as distinguished from the continental United States.

The fifty States *accepted the benefits (bribes) offered* by the federal UNITED STATES *as consideration for the commercial agreements* that bind each of the corporate States to the Federal UNITED STATES. The corporate States are now obligated to obey the Congress of the federal UNITED STATES and assume their portion of the equitable debts of the federal UNITED STATES owed to the international banks for the credit borrowed from the bankers. The credit that each State receives, *in the form of federal grants,* is predicated upon equitable, paper debts.

This system of negotiable paper binds all corporate entities together in a vast system of commercial agreements that have altered our courts from under the common law to *legislative Article I Courts of commercial law.*

Persons brought before this court are held to the letter of every statute on the federal, state, county, or municipal levels *unless they have exercised the REMEDY provided for them by law . . .* whereby, when *forced* to use a "benefit" provided to them by the government *they may reserve their rights not to be bound by any commercial agreement or silent contract that they did not enter knowingly, willingly, and intentionally, with full disclosure of the facts.*

In 1976 Congress took away all semblance of common law that remained in the courts. *All law today is construed and constructed by the judge as it happens in his court.* Common law has almost disappeared from the courts. They took away any control we might have over the courts, and *this has been hidden from us all.*

Many patriots, in courts today, wonder how the courts can override the laws the patriots put in their paperwork. It's simple. *The judges construe and construct the law as they will.*

A simple word change such as "in" to "at" as in "at law" or "in law" gives a totally different meaning.

For example: If you're **in** the river you are wet, you can swim, etc. But if you're **at** the river you might enjoy a picnic, play ball, or run a race. See the difference a **word-of-art** can make? Attorneys often change this word — and others — when they answer motions.

It will pay you to read the answers of attorneys to your paperwork. Compare what they say that case law says, with the actual case law itself. You'll discover that they often changed the words therein.

This is illegal, you might say! No! Not according to the US Code.

They can construe and construct any statute to mean what they want it to mean for their benefit. You are not aware of this. You think you are being railroaded in a kangaroo court.

No! *They are legal in what they do. They (usually) follow the law, to the letter of the law — their **private** law — the law of silent contracts that you know nothing about.*

This is the nature of *contract law.*

16

The UCC:
Contract, Acceptance & Dishonor

If you don't understand contract law or realize what law you are dealing with when you go into court, you will lose. Even if you have filed your UCC-1 Finance Statement (Declaration) and have redeemed your real name and your artificial entity strawman, this makes no difference in Article I, commercial law courts. Why? Because they operate in total fiction, *in the land of Oz.*

They can only recognize *contracts.* And you are a *real sentient being,* having numerous *adhesion contracts* attached to you.

Whatever you file in that court, whether it is your UCC-1 Finance Statement, or law from the judicial and original, jurisdiction side that is real, lawful, and the true; *they do not recognize what is true, they only recognize fictions and contract law.*

So, when you go into any court, be aware that it is *their* law, and the judge or the prosecutor can *construe and construct* that law in any way he chooses, and it will always mean what he *chooses* it to mean.

Contracts supercede constitutional common law.

The courts are not bound by the Constitution or common law. They are bound only by *contracts,* and the statutes used to enforce those contracts that are made.

When used in conjunction with one's signature, a stamp stating *"Without Prejudice"* or *"All Rights Reserved"* is sufficient to indicate to the magistrate of any of our Legislative

Tribunals (*called "courts"*) that the signer of the document has *reserved his common law right* to not be bound to any statute, or commercial obligation, or agreement that *he did not enter knowingly, willingly, voluntarily, and intentionally,* for such is the case in any common law contract.

Furthermore, pursuant to UCC 1-103, the statute being enforced as the *commercial obligation* of an agreement, *must be construed in harmony with the common law of America* whereby the court must rule that the statute does not apply to the individual who is *informed enough* to exercise the *Remedy* provided in this new system of law.

He retains his former status in the Republic, and fully enjoys his ***un-a-lien-able rights*** that the Constitution for the united States for America guarantees, even for those who lack the truth needed to free themselves from *slave status* under the DISTRICT OF COLUMBIA UNITED STATES.

17

Summation of History

Development of Modern Feudalism

THE UNITED STATES is a corporation created in England that comes under the jurisdiction of the Crown. This entitles England to create laws, and establish those laws in THE UNITED STATES. And everyone who is a 14th Amendment Citizen of the commercial UNITED STATES is subject to obey those laws.

This places the Congress of the COMMERCIAL UNITED STATES *above what we think of as the Constitution.* The only "Bill of Rights" left to the 14th Amendment Citizen are the 13th, 14th 15th, and 16th Amendments. These are the only amendments to the Constitution that the courts are required to recognize when you appear in court.

The 1929 stock market crash, and the Great Depression that followed, placed the American people in desperation, homelessness, poverty, and starvation. The people were focused on *survival* at that time. They were *conditioned* to accept any handout the government offered them, regardless of the cost to their freedoms.

We were drawn in as *14th Amendment Citizens* through the registration of our birth certificates. We were *further* enticed into that system by volunteering for many other licenses and privileges offered to us by the government as *peace offerings* to enemies of the commercial UNITED STATES. *This act gave the UNITED STATES INC., total authority over us as a conquered people under the laws of war,* to force anything on us they might choose to create.

Then in 1976, Congress removed any and all semblance of justice in our court system with Senate bill, 94-201 and 94-381. From this point on, *"officers of the court" could "construe and construct" the law to mean anything they choose it to mean.*

As 14th Amendment Citizens, we are not citizens of the America we have always thought we knew. *We are citizens of England through the incorporation of THE UNITED STATES under English law.* There is no American *law* today, only copyrighted statutes interpreted by "judges" who *"construe and construct"* whatever they decide those statutes to mean.

As "Soverans" we *unknowingly* recognized the Crown of England — the IMF — as the Principle Creditor of THE UNITED STATES.

The creditor of the corporate UNITED STATES is the IMF, never you, or me.

The Creditor of the UNITED STATES installed *invisible* contracts to ensnare the sovereign people of America as its subjects. The Creditor of THE UNITED STATES implemented the *invisible* contracts through apparent *"color of law"* and we "Soverans" *unknowingly* agreed. We as Soverans, via the invisible contracts and our lack of responsibility to reject the creditor's (the IMF's) ideas, *are voluntarily giving our substance to the mythical creator of this ruse.*

There is a common thread woven throughout our entire history, and that is *commerce! the merchant, the money-changer (the banks), the law merchant,* i.e., the law of commerce, civil and maritime admiralty law.

This is not to say that commerce is bad; it does however

say that commerce (like the strawman of OZ) brings with it the unthinking laws of commerce.

Wherever commerce goes, it brings laws that can bind people into slavery. But this can happen only if we the people agree.

Banks create "money" today out of thin air and charge us interest on their creation. *But this can happen only if we the people agree.*

The merchants and the bankers create laws, through lawmakers whom they control, who protect commerce and bind the people to obey. *But this can happen only if we the people agree.*

The only reason this occurs is that we do not handle our own affairs and rely on somebody else to handle them for us.

Reclaim Your Sovereignty

18

Me & My Shadow -
My Fictional Strawman

The elected and appointed administrators of the government of the United States have been filing certified copies of our Birth Records in the United States Department of Commerce, as Registered Securities.

These securities, each of which carries an estimated $1,000,000 (*one million dollar*) value, and are circulated around the world as collateral for loans, entries on the asset side of ledgers, etc., just like any other Security.

There's just one problem — we didn't authorize it.

Now that you know this, you can *take back* (*redeem*) *your* sovereignty and name — or continue to let the government use you and them as collateral to pay the interest on the federal debt to the Crown.

The United States is a *District of Columbia corporation.* In Volume 20 of *Corpus Juris,* Section 1785, we find *"The United States government is a foreign corporation with respect to a State." — N.Y. re: Merriam 36 N.E. 505 1441 S. 0.1973, 14 L. Ed. 287.*

Since a corporation is a fictitious, "legal person" that *cannot speak, see, touch, smell, or taste, etc.,* it cannot function in the real world by itself. It needs a conduit, a "transmitting utility," a *liaison* of some sort to "connect" the fictitious person, from the fictional world in which *it* exists, to the real person and the real world in which *he* lives.

In other words . . .

Living people exist in the real world, not in a fictional, virtual world. *But government exists in a fictional world and can only deal directly with other fictional persons, agencies, corporations, states, etc.* In order for a *fictional* person to deal with a *real* person there must be a connection, a liaison, a go-between. This can be something as simple as an agreement or a contract.

When both "persons" (both the real and fictional) agree to the terms of a contract, there is *a connection, interchange, intercourse, dealings, there is communication, an exchange, there is business.*

But there is *another* way for fictional government to deal with the real live woman and man — *through the use of a representative, an agent, a liaison, a go-between.*

Who is this go-between that connects fictional government to the real man? *It's a government-created shadow, a fictional Strawman . . . a* **corporation of one** with the same name as yours, but printed in the ALL CAPS name of a corporation.

This "person" was created by using your birth certificate as the Manufacturer's Certificate of Origin (MCO) and the State in which you were born as the Port of Entry (POE) onto the fictional venue. This gave the fictional UNITED STATES a fictional PERSON with whom it can deal directly. *This "person" is your* **ens legis** (meaning government created) *fictional strawman.*

stramineus homo: Latin - A man of straw, one of no substance put forward as bail or surety — *Black's Law Dictionary, 6th Edition, page 1421.*

Following the definition of *stramineus homo* in Black's we find the next word, *strawman.*

strawman: *A fictitious person,* esp. one that is weak or flawed. A front. *A third party* used in some transactions as a temporary transferee to allow the principal parties to accomplish something that is otherwise impermissible. *A nominal party* to a transaction, one who acts as an agent for another for the purpose of taking title to real property and executing whatever documents and instruments the principal may direct. *A person* who purchases property for another to conceal the identity of the real purchaser or to accomplish some purpose otherwise not allowed.

Webster's Ninth New Collegiate Dictionary defines the term "strawman" as "a weak or imaginary opposition set up only to be easily confuted; or a person set up to serve as a cover for a usually questionable transaction".

The Strawman can be summed up as a passive, imaginary stand-in for the real participant; a front; a blind; a person regarded as a nonentity. *The Strawman is a **shadow go-between.***

A man or woman's name written in ALL CAPS, or last name first, does not identify a real live person. The rules of grammar for the English language have no provisions for the abbreviation of one's name, *i.e. initials are not to be used.*

As an example, **John Adam Smith** is correct. Anything else is not correct.

Not Smith, John Adam, or Smith, John A. or J. Smith, or J.A. Smith, or JOHN ADAM SMITH, or SMITH, JOHN, or any other variation. Nothing, other than **John Adam Smith** identifies the real, living man. All other *appellations* identify either a deceased man or a fictitious man such as a corporation or strawman.

Over the years, the government — through its "public" school system — has managed to pull the wool over our eyes and keep us ignorant of some most important facts. Because all facets of the media have an ever increasing influence in our lives, and because the media are controlled by government. and its agencies (*by licenses, etc.*), we have slowly, and systematically been conditioned to believe that any *form of our name* (appellation) is in fact us as long as the spelling is correct. This is not true.

We were never told, with full and open disclosure, what our government officials were planning to do, and why.

We were never told, that the government (*THE UNITED STATES*) is a corporation, a fictitious "person".

We were never told, that the government had quietly, almost secretly, created a shadow corporation, a fictional strawman for each and every American, so that the government could not only control the people, *but also raise an almost unlimited amount of revenue, so it could continue not just to exist but to grow.*

We were never told, that when the government deals with the strawman it is not dealing with real, living men and women.

We were never told, with full disclosure of all of the facts, that *since June 5, 1933 we have been unable to pay our debts.*

We were never told, that we and our children, and their children and their children's children *have been pledged as collateral (mere chattel) for the debt created by government officials who commit treason in doing so.*

We were never told, that they quietly and cleverly *changed the rules, even the game itself,* and that the world we perceive of as real, is in fact fictional, and its all for their benefit.

We were never told, *that the strawman* — a fictional person created by the State — *is subject to all the codes, statutes, rules, regulations, ordinances, etc. decreed by government . . .* but that we, the real, living man and woman, are not.

We were never told, that we were being treated as property, as slaves (albeit comfortably for some) while living in the land of the free, *and that we could easily walk away from the fraud.*

We were never told, that we were being abused.

By knowing the difference between our real self and our strawman, and by behaving accordingly, *we regain our sovereignty over "legal fictions," and the ability to experi-ence* **the true freedom that is our birthright**, *for the freedom of the divinity in us all.*

Something else we should know: ever since June 1933 everything operates in commerce.

Why is this important? *Commerce is based on agree-ments . . .* **on contracts**.

The Government has an *implied* agreement with your strawman, which they created, subject to government rule. But when we *voluntarily assume* that they are trying to communicate with *us,* and *step into their commercial "pro-cess,"* we become the "Surety" (*Co-signer*) for their fic-tional Strawman.

Reality and fiction are then reversed.

We become liable for the debts, liabilities and obligations of the Strawman, relinquishing our real (protected by the Constitution) character, as we "stand-in" for their fictional Strawman.

So that we can once again place the STRAWMAN in the fictional world, and keep ourselves in the real world (*with all our "shields" in place against the fictional government*), we can send a **non-negotiable Charge Back** and a **non-negotiable Bill of Exchange** to the Secretary of the Treasury of the United States along with a **certified copy of our birth certificate,** the Manufacturer's Certificate of Origin (MCO) of our *ens legis* (*government created*) strawman.

When you hold the title to your Strawman and anyone else makes a claim against "him or it," *it is a commercial trespass.* If anyone goes after your fictional Strawman and wins any *monetary award* against the fictional Strawman, *then you* (*the real person, the **Secured Party Creditor***) *get the first $1,000,000* (*one million dollars*) *of that monetary award* because you have the **priority first lien** against "him or it," *the strawman.*

It's all business, a commercial undertaking, and the basic procedure is not complicated. In fact it's fairly simple. We simply have to remember a few things. *This is not a "legal" procedure. We're not playing "People's Court".* This is **commerce** and we play by the rules of commerce.

We accept the claim (*"Agree with thine adversary quickly." - Matt. 5:25*) and become the holder in due course of the claim, and challenge whether or not the presenter of the claim has the proper authority to make the claim (*to charge our account*) in the first place. When they cannot produce the *order* (*they never can, it was never issued*) we request that the account be properly adjusted, *and the charge or claim goes away.*

Always Accept for Value the claim. Become the **Holder-in-due-course** of the claim. Decide not to prosecute yourself.

If they don't adjust the account, *you can request the bookkeeping records showing where the funds in question were assigned.* Request the *Fiduciary Tax Estimate* and the *Fiduciary Tax Return* for this claim.

Since you have *accepted the claim for value* and it is *pre-paid,* your UCC, Contract Insurance Trust Account (CITA) is exempt from levy, and the request for the *Fiduciary Tax Estimate* and the *Fiduciary Tax Return* is valid because this information is necessary to determine who is delinquent and making claims on your account.

If there is no record of the *Fiduciary Tax Estimate* and the *Fiduciary Tax Return, request the individual tax estimates and individual tax returns* to determine if there is a delinquency.

If you receive no favorable response to the above requests, *you can file a currency report on the amount claimed against your insurance account* and begin the commercial process that will force them either to do what is required, or lose everything they own. *This is the power of contracts in commerce.*

A contract overrides the Constitution, the Bill of Rights, or any other document, other than a superior contract.

No "color of law" under the present codes, statutes, rules, regulations, ordinances, etc., can operate upon you.

No agent and-or government agency, including courts, can gain jurisdiction over you, *without your consent.* You do not exist within their commercial fictional venue, *unless you join it.*

The **Acceptance for Value Process** (AVP) gives you the ability to deal with claimants *through the use of your transmitting utility, go-between strawman,* to hold the claimant accountable in his own commercial world for any action he attempts to take against you.

Without a proper order (*and we know they're not in possession of such a document*) they must leave you alone, or pay the consequences.

In addition to reclaiming your freedom, you remove your collateral from the frauds, manipulations, and extortions that have been perpetrated in your name.

When enough people have **reclaimed their birthright,** we will be able to reclaim the Constitutional Republic that was intended to protect our life our liberty and pursuit of happiness.

But the **Acceptance for Value Process** (AVP) is not for everyone. *If you don't understand what you're doing, don't do it. You can get into serious trouble, if you administer it wrongly.*

You can't learn the process all at once. "Rome wasn't built in a day."

19
Summary

All law is Private Merchantile Law, making the people Sureties and Debtors of the bankruptcy of the DISTRICT OF COLUMBIA UNITED STATES.

Universal law is contract. So we must follow the progression of the contractual agreements that constitute the underlying UNITED STATES law.

No one person can address all the laws, statutes, and cases that exist. However, *"Ignorance of the law is no excuse."* Therefore, the following progression of contracts and our interpretation of them, follows in basically, chronological order:

*THE UNITED STATES OF AMERICA is a bankrupt corporation of the English Crown, and has been since 1788. **Article 12** of the Articles of Confederation state that:*

"All bills of credit emitted, monies borrowed, and debts contracted by, or under the authority of Congress, before the assembling of the United States, in pursuance of the present confederation, shall be deemed as considered *a charge against the United States, for payment and satisfaction* whereof the said United States *and the public faith* are hereby solemnly pledged."

As *Constitutors,* the "Founding Fathers acknowledged their debt to the Crown, and constitutionalized it in 1787 in Article VI of the Constitution.

A *constitutor* is a person who by agreement becomes responsible for another's debt. (*Blacks Law 7th, p.307*).

The bankruptcy resulted from twenty-one loans that the Founding Fathers borrowed from the Crown of England between February 28, 1778 and July 5, 1782 to help finance the Revolutionary War. The loans were ratified by Congress, for six more years, on January 22, 1783, *four years prior to the Constitution.*

When Congress foresaw that they wouldn't be able to repay the loans in 1788, when they were due, Congress convened a convention, *to make a constitutum.*

A *constitutum* is an agreement to pay ones own, or another's, existing debt. (ibid).

The *constitutum* gave the Crown a mortgage on the new States which they ratified two years later in 1789.

Congress chartered the private United States Bank, in 1791, with England owning 18,000 (72%) of the 25,000 total shares of the bank.

No constitutional Congress has existed since March 27, 1861 when seven southern States walked out of Congress, leaving it without a quorum for adjourning and without calling a time and a date to reconvene, ending *sine die* ('*without day*').

What is *called* Congress today *functions under the authority of the President acting as the Commander-In-Chief of the Armed Forces under emergency, war-powers rule,* the law of necessity, which equals *no law. — See 12 Stat 319* which has never been repealed, at *Title 50 USC §§ 212, 213, 215, Appendix 16, 26 CFR Chapter 1 § 303.1-6(a) and 31 CFR Chapter 5 § 500.701 Penalties.*

Americans have been under fascist rule via presidential executive order under emergency war powers since March 27, 1861. — 12 USC 95(a)(b).

Every citizen of the united States of America is an "enemy" of THE UNITED STATES via the Amendatory Act of March 9, 1933. — 48 Stat. 1, amending Trading With Enemy Act of October 6, 1917, H.R. 4960, Public Law No. 91.

On December 6th, 1868, the 14th Amendment was proclaimed to be ratified, *even though it never was.* The 14th Amendment is a constructive, *cestui que* trust, a private Roman Catholic, ecclesiastical trust law. *A public, charitable trust designed to bring every corporate franchise, called a "citizen of the United States, Inc.," into an inseparable partnership with the United States, Inc.,* making the two entities one, with all power inhering in the government, instead of the people.

A *cestui que trust* is different from a *regular* trust.

A **regular** trust is made up of the contractual indenture of three parties: 1. **the executor** of the trust (*the grantor; the creator of the trust; the trustor*), 2. **the trustee(s)**, and (3) **the beneficiary(ies)**.

In a **regular** trust, legal ownership is transferred by a *written contract* between the grantor and the trustees in which the grantor surrenders ownership of property to the *"legal person"* (the Trust) to be managed by the trustees on behalf of the beneficiaries.

A *cestui que trust* differs from a regular *trust* in two ways:

1. *a cestui que trust* is not formed by an open agreement expressed in writing, *but by fiat legal*

construction instead of by a grantor.

2. *a cestui que trust* has no grantor. *It is a constructive trust created by law (by fiat; by make-believe). It has only beneficiaries and trustees.* It is the **trustee(s)'** duty to manage the property of the **beneficiary(ies)** . . . *"for the public good."*

The Legislative Act of February 21, 1871, 41st Congress, Session III, Chapter 62, page 419, chartered a federal *corporation* called "United States," a commercial agency that was originally called "Washington, D.C." in accordance with the 14th Amendment that the record indicates was never ratified. — *Utah Supreme Court Cases, Dyett v Turner, (1968) 439 P2d 266, 267 . . . State v Phillips, (1975) 540 P 2d 936 . . . as well as Coleman v. Miller, 307 U.S. 448, 59 S. Ct. 972 . . . 28 Tulane Law Review, 22 . . . 11 South Carolina Law Quarterly 484 . . . Congressional Record, June 13, 1967, pp. 15641-15646.*

A Citizen of the UNITED STATES *is civilly dead*, operating as a co-trustee of the public, charitable trust, the constructive, *cestui que trust* of THE UNITED STATES INC., under the 14th Amendment which supports the debt of THE UNITED STATES INC., to the Crown referred to in the Constitution, in Section 4.

SECTION 4. The validity of the public debt of the United States . . . shall not be questioned.

To conform to the 1871 creation of the commercial UNITED STATES and the 14th Amendment, the Legislature of each State created by charter a limited-liability corporation in a *private, military, international, commercial, admiralty-maritime jurisdictional venue* entitled "STATE OF (whatever state)…" e.g. "STATE OF MAINE" as evidenced by *inter alia* (*among other things*) the change in the Seal and the creation of a New Constitution, e.g. "Constitution of the State of Maine" concerning which regarding Maine:

1. A general partnership agreement (*hereinafter "General Partnership"*) exists between the Maine Republic and STATE OF MAINE with the STATE OF MAINE acting as Governmental controller of the partnership.

2. STATE OF MAINE now acts as an agent/instrumentality of the UNITED STATES collecting *whole life insurance premiums* called "taxes" for the International Monetary Fund (IMF) based *inter alia* upon the Limited Liability Act of 1851 and the bankruptcy of the United States of 1933.

(See House Joint Resolution 192 of June 5, 1933; Public Law 73-10; and Perry v. U.S. (1935), 294 U.S. 330-381, 79 L Ed 912; 31 USC 5112, 5119).

The contract involved in a constructive trust is an implied contract. An implied contract can be ratified by one of the two following means:

1. ***Acquiescence by silence,*** i.e. when the "government" asserts its intentions concerning your life, rights, and property and you don't rebut its assertions and compliantly go along with what they claim, you assent (*agree*).

In 1871 the Government changed the nature of its Contract with the people from law — *as defined by the original Constitution of 1787 that recognizes common law* — to maritime admiralty (*on the sea only*) and equity (*functioning by voluntary contract between all participating parties*), and began relating to the people as if they were "Citizens of THE UNITED STATES" (*within and under the private, commercial, international, military jurisdiction of the new de facto corporation, i.e. the UNITED STATES INC.*).

The government offered the people a "New Deal" and almost everyone bought into it based on naive and foolish trust and the assumption that everything was OK. The people were thereby denied access to law and placed on the Ship of State (*U.S. INC.*) wherein the Captain's word is law and no one has any rights, *only privileges.*

As Jefferson phrased the matter, *"As government grows liberty recedes."*

2. **expressly accepting the benefits offered** and therefor binding the contract by one's actions and deeds.

This is similar to binding a contract with a restaurant owner by sitting down at a table, reading a menu, and then ordering and consuming a meal.

By your deeds you affirm to the restaurant owner that you will pay for the meal in accordance with the price stated on the menu.

No written contract is signed, but *a cestui que trust contract is formed and bound,* nevertheless.

By the above two means, the people unknowingly give their implied assent to be bound by an implied contract with

THE UNITED STATES INC. in accordance with the terms and conditions that inhere in being treated as a citizen of THE UNITED STATES under the 14th Amendment, and are therefore placed into the position of involuntary servitude as a debtor and surety of THE UNITED STATES INC. In such a position people loose the status of sovereignty and their capacity to assert their unalienable rights and are presumed to have exercised their autonomous *sovereign-free-will* for the purpose of accepting the government's presumption that they will sacrifice everything for the "public good" . . . for the public charitable trust. By so doing the people loose their standing in law, they *"die a civil death in the law."*

They are placed in the legal position of *mortmain* (*as if deceased*) and are stripped of their capacity for asserting their rights, since the presumption is that *they have already exercised their rights for the purpose of agreeing with the position they are in, as property of the government, with a lien against them and everything their labor has and will ever create, including their children.* The private individual (*the real flesh and blood person*) is sacrificed "for the good of the State," *the imaginary collective.*

When people die such a "civil death" in the law, they are like ghosts who are thereby *incapable of managing their own affairs and enjoying their unalienable rights.* Like the estate of a decedent, *they are then managed by the executor-administrator of their estate, in a probate court.*

Such is the condition of *every* citizen in law of THE UNITED STATES today, managed by government agencies acting as *executors and administrators of their estates* in bankruptcy, legal incapacity, and civil death, as assets of the bankrupt UNITED STATES.

THE UNITED STATES belongs to the *private, **real parties of interest*** . . . the actual Creditors of the bankruptcy.

The 14th Amendment was created for the purpose of establishing citizenship for *the newly liberated blacks and other disenfranchised people who could not otherwise comply with the requirements for citizenship in the State.*

What actually happened was that the blacks were taken off the southern plantations and placed in the Plantation of the UNITED STATES INC., a far worse lot.

The government then gradually encompassed **everyone else** into the same status and state of **involuntary feudal servitude.**

20

Accept for Value & Return
Discharge or Payment / Settlement & Closure

A fictional government functions only in a fictional world, in a world where there is no money, only fictional funds, mere entries; figures; digits.

All charges consist of negative commercial claims against your Strawman; not against you. Numbers are moved from one side of the ledger account to the other side as credits and debits.

Resisting these charges only gets us into trouble; so we accept them and discharge the charge with FRNs and thereby balance the account, or we can "pay" the charge with a UCC mutual offset credit exemption exchange.

Accepting the charge removes the controversy. So there is nothing to adjudicate; nothing to go court for, *unless you let it.*

Acceptance for Value (accepting the charge for its value to us) removes the negative claim against the Strawman's account and we becoming the Holder-in-due-course of the charge/presentment/claim, and can order that the account be adjusted to zero, via our promissory note.

Only *we* can balance the account, because only *we* have the power to issue our credit, via our promissory note. All debt is created on paper; therefore all debt can be discharged or paid with other pieces of paper.

Playing the commercial game allows us to control the movement of figures, digits, and entries into the account, for *our* benefit instead of the benefit of those who would confiscate our labor in the form of cash.

Now statutes, codes, rules, regulations no longer apply to us; they apply only to the Strawman whom we now own and control. Now the Feds have no jurisdiction over us, because they do not have our consent, nor are we in their fictional domain. Those of us who *choose* to take charge of our commercial affairs become part of the solution instead of remaining part of the problem.

In order to get one's independence back, one must first secure the title and ownership to his Strawman. Once he controls his Strawman, he controls the rights to the property that the Strawman acquires and owns.

For one to regain title to his body, the Birth Certificate must be secured. After we have redeemed it and filed public notice via a UCC financing statement, for our "transmitting utility," we have the right of property ownership through our Strawman whom we now own and control. The bond created and sold in the market place for the Strawman, and the interest it accrues, now become *our* property, instead of *his and the State's.*

Think of the board game Monopoly where you pick up a Chance card which reads, "Pay School Tax $150." So you hand over the $$$ to the Banker. (*I think the Parker boys were trying to tell us something*).

When the government charges the Strawman a tax *we,* the ostensible "players" are held as "surety" for our Token/Strawman and are "required to pay," even though the charge is not directed towards us. The charge is directed towards our *token* (*our Strawman; the Top Hat, Race Car, or Old Shoe*). We are paying *for the token* because our token isn't real, so it can't *do anything by itself. We* provide the energy and act for our Token/Strawman.

Since the money is also not real, there could be no real *loss* to us as natural beings, except that this *seems* to be all there is.

We used to be able to live a *real* life with *real* money. Now we are playing a commercial game with "Monopoly" money instead. We have been prevented from living a real life; we are caught in the game. This did *not* come about by our conscious consent.

What if we want to go back to living a real life? We'd have to get out of the game.

This is tricky because the 'powers-that-be' are able to control us by confiscating our finances to keep us in the game. Why would they allow us to opt out of a game that they are sure to win; which we are destined to lose?

There is no way to stop playing the game unless we consciously do what it takes in order to extricate ourselves from the game. It is simple, but not easy, mostly because the banksters and their lawyers refuse to lose. Also, most of us don't realize that we *have* a choice, because *most* have never considered that we unknowingly **agree** to play the game; a game we can't win.

Would **anyone** consciously choose to play such a game? I think not.

The UCC is the rule book of the game, and any entity within the game is *corporate,* since no living soul can play this game, only Strawmen. Only *documented* (registered) entities can play the game. Therefore, the Income Tax Act, *being part of the Commerce Game,* applies only to fictitious entities, as they are the *only* registered entities who can play in the game.

Because the name of the game is **"confiscation of funds,"** they hold **us** (we who want only to live life as freely as possible and 'not infringe upon the rights of another') as surety for our Strawman's alleged debt. But Public Policy — HJR 192 of June 5, 1933 ("Order in Council" of April 10, 1933, in Canada) — tells us that as there is no substance with which to "pay" a debt, so all debt **can be discharged.**

How can we "pay" a debt when there is nothing of substance with which to "pay." We can't "pay" a debt with money, since there is no real money in circulation today. The only thing left is our credit. So we can "pay" the Strawman's debt with our credit. ***With our UCC mutual offset credit exemption exchange.***

For more discrete information in this regard see Lessons 20 and 21 in . . .

New Beginning Study Course: Connect The Dots
And See
<u>http://tinyurl.com/yc4jkyd</u>

How is our credit created? VIA OUR SIGNATURE.

Every time we sign our name to any promissory note we create credit. So we must certainly have a lot of credit. Are we using it? Or is some public entity using it instead? Every time we sign our name for any commercial purpose, to any public entity, we are giving away our credit exemption exchange. But what are we getting in return?

Example: If you go through a Stop sign, it is not you who is charged; your Strawman is charged, because it is his/its name on the driver licence which you carry around and unwittingly use as your "identification" instead of his/it's identification.

Also, any citation is directed to the Strawman; it does not have *your* name on it. However, since the Strawman doesn't exist except on paper, it is *you* who are held as surety for the fine. Slick game; right? Right.

I hear you saying, **"but it was I who broke the law by going through the Stop sign."**

What law?

Remember: there is no *"law"* other than the one which protects the life, liberty, rights, and property of all living souls. So, you didn't break any "law," unless someone were injured, in which case, as an honorable soul, you would make restitution somehow.

To this end you might post a bond with the Secretary of State in the event of an incident in which you might have to compensate another human being. We should *not* have to pay a federally-owned corporation called an *insurance agent* to "protect" us — to protect us from the Protectors. The bond would be backed by our exemption which is un-limited.

Which is better . . . a slave laboring to pay an insurance premium to an entity which might not cover your transgres-sions or might cancel your policy on a whim . . . or backing any possible commercial liability with your own unlimited exemption via a surety bond? I say the *latter* is better and safer.

Soon we could provide 'insurance' for one another.

In former times, when a farmer's barn burned down his neighbors assisted him in rebuilding it, based upon their anticipation of some day needing assistance *themselves* from neighboring farmers "good will."

The banksters infiltrated this workable plan by creating

an insurance *industry* in the same manner they infiltrated the people's *trade* by creating a debt-money system, saying:

"You now have to use our money and insurance companies instead of relying upon yourselves and your neighbors; but its going to cost you . . ."

Who fell for this? Why would *anyone* want to put the credit of his trust into a fictional entity when he has trusted his neighbors for decades?

Back to the traffic case.

What act occurred for which you are being held for the charge against your Strawman? You violated a statute. The statute applies only to *fictitious* entities. And since a *Strawman* can't do anything let alone stop at a Stop sign, the traffic cop (*who might know this*) will cause you to *believe* that it is *you* who made the transgression.

But no statute applies to living souls, any more than "Go to jail; go directly to jail; do not pass GO; do NOT collect $200" in Monopoly applies to *you*; it applies to the *Token, race car.*

Too many of us live in fear. This fear translates into $$$ for someone else.

I've asked people of all ages if they could have what they want, what would that be? They generally respond, *"More money."* When people have what they believe to be a 'problem,' they tend to want to fix the **effect** as opposed to the **cause.** They talk about getting a second job or getting another member of the family out to work, or borrowing $$$, in order to 'make ends meet'.

Did any of these frantic individuals ever sit down and ask, **"*Why* don't we have enough $$$?"** If they did, the answer they would come up with is that we are *programed* with every day, which is:

"Americans are spending way beyond their means and going into serious debt."

This answer is utterly FALSE.

Most feel guilt because they believe **themselves** to be the cause of the problem, they do what they can to put a "BandAid" upon the *effect,* instead of investigating the **cause.**

NONE of what you have been led to believe about "national" or "personal debt" is true. You have been conned by the *masterminds* of the banks. Bear in mind; this is ALL by design — a brilliant design to confiscate the property, land, cash, assets, and the intrinsic value of the people of the world — our labor — for the main purpose of mental and bodily control !

Reclaim Your Sovereignty

"Surely in vain the net is spread in the sight of any bird." — Proverbs 1:17.

Reclaim Your Sovereignty

"As we have borne the image of the earthy, we shall also bear the image of the heavenly."
— 1 Corinthians 15:49.

Reclaim Your Sovereignty

PROMISSORY NOTE PACKAGE

AUTHOR'S RENDITION

Dear Payee (2nd Party)

THE FEDERAL RESERVE BANK OF NEW YORK states that:

"Money does not have to be issued by a govern-ment or be in any special form."

THE FEDERAL RESERVE BANK OF NEW YORK
PUBLICATION "I BET YOU THOUGHT"

Article IX of the Bill of Rights states that:

"The enumeration in the Constitution of certain rights shall not be construed to deny or disparage others retained by the people."

THEREFORE, I, _____, a Secured Party Creditor of the federal corporate UNITED STATES, believe and certify in good faith, under the authority of Article IX of the Bill of Rights, that the right to issue Bills of Credit and to declare the same to be legal tender for the payment of all UNLAWFUL public or private debts has been by the People RETAINED.

Refusal of this lawfully tendered promissory note places the refuser in contempt of Congress and in dishonor of Public Policy HJR-192 of 1933.

CERTIFIED PROMISSORY MONEY NOTE
IN GOD WE TRUST

No. _____

Date _____

THIS PROMISSORY NOTE IS A UCC NEGOTIABLE INSTRU-
MENT REDEEMABLE AT FULL FACE VALUE WHEN PRE-
SENTED TO THE ENS LEGIS ISSUER AT HIS ADDRESS.
VOID IF NOT PRESENTED FOR PAYMENT WITHIN SIX (6)
MONTHS. THIS NOTE IS LEGAL TENDER FOR THE PAY-
MENT OF ALL UNLAWFUL DEBTS.

THE UNDERSIGNED WILL PAY TO THE ORDER

OF_____

Payee (2nd party)

_____ DOLLARS

of "Money of Account of the United States" as required by law at 31 USC 371 / from the
time of the official determination of the substance of said money or of UCC 1-201(24)
credit money.

_____

AUTHORIZED SIGNATURE CERTIFYING ACCEPTANCE & PAYMENT

_____

ENS LEGIS NAME IN ALL CAPS

_____

ENS LEGIS ADDRESS IN ALL CAPS

_____

ENS LEGIS LOCATION IN ALL CAPS

ISSUER AND PAYOR: FIRST PARTY / ENS LEGIS

Take Back Your Christian Name   115

Administrative Notice

Under the laws of equity, the UNITED STATES cannot **hypothecate and re-hypothecate** the private property and wealth of its private citizens and put them at risk as collateral for its **fiat currency and credit obligations** to the Federal Reserve Bank without providing the private citizens of America with a lawful equitable **REMEDY** for recovery of interest on their risk that is due and payable to them upon demand.

The UNITED STATES does not violate the law because the UNITED STATES provides the sovereign citizens of America with a legal **REMEDY** for the recovery of what is due them as **accrued interest** on the use and risk of their assets and wealth so that it can legally **hypothecate and re-hypothecate** the private wealth and assets of the people to the Federal Reserve Bank to back its fiat currency and debt obligations with their material substance, credit and implied consent.

The provisions for this **REMEDY** are found in **Public (insurance) Policy HJR-192 of 1933 i.e. Public Law 73-10.**

All UNITED STATES fiat currency since 1933 represents **CREDIT** backed by the real property, wealth, assets and future labor of the sovereign people of America that the UNITED STATES has **taken by presumptive pledge** and **re-pledged** as a **secondary obligation** to the non-federal Federal Reserve Bank.

The attorneys who devise the public laws and regulations Congress rubber-stamps that orchestrate **the bankruptcy reorganization** of the corporate UNITED STATES anticipated the long term inflationary effect of its **debt based monetary system** that many in government feared so they made statutory provisions for this **REMEDY** to provide **equity-interest recovery-payment** to their Sureties (sovereign Americans), and at the same time payments on National Debt.

Since the real property, wealth and assets of all Americans is the **faith and substance** that backs the obligations, fiat currency and credit of the UNITED STATES, such credit has been **tacitly offered** and can be **accepted and used** for **equity-interest recovery** via **mutual offset credit exemption exchange.**

Public Policy HJR-192 of 1933 provides for the **discharge** of every debt obligation of the federal UNITED STATES and its sub-divisions by **discharging dollar for dollar** the obligations that are owed them against the same dollar for dollar amounts that the UNITED STATES owes us, thus providing this **REMEDY** for **equity-interest recovery** and the eventual payoff of the public (National) debt.

"The public debt is that portion of the total federal debt that is held by the public." (31 USC 1230).

Public Policy HJR-192 of 1933 and 31 USC 5103 gives private unincorporated people (the Secured Party Creditors of the federal UNITED STATES) the right to issue legal tender promissory notes **"upon the full faith and credit of the UNITED STATES"** as obligations of the federal UNITED STATES to them.

This **REMEDY** for the recovery of **equity-interest via mutual offset credit exemption exchange** is codified in statutory law although this benefit is virtually unknown by the people and therefore seldom utilized in commerce today.

Federal Reserve Notes are promissory notes of debt that Congress has promised to **redeem** for us with offsets of credit upon our demand.

A bill is a demand for payment in **real "money of account of the United States"** that cannot be made because there is no **real**

"money of account of the United States" in use today with which to pay one. **Federal Reserve Notes discharge** and our **personal credit pays** debt instead.

Our personal credit (our promise to pay) pays debt when we accept a bill for its value **with our promissory note endorsement** and return its value to the sender to offset, zero and balance the sender's account.

Using Federal Reserve Notes is optional whether we know it or not.

HJR-192 of 1933 did not *order* people **to use Federal Reserve Notes to discharge debts,** it simply *allows* them to use them if they choose to do so.

People use Federal Reserve Notes voluntarily whether they know it or not.

Since there is no **real "money of account of the United States,"** a **monetary charge** is an **offer to contract** to settle the debt with either **Federal Reserve Notes** or with one's **mutual offset credit exemption exchange.**

A debtor has the option of *discharging* his debts **with Federal Reserve Notes,** — or *paying* his debts **with his mutual offset credit exemption exchange** . . . via his

PROMISSORY NOTE.

"UCC TRANSMITTING UTILITY"
DECLARATION OF REDEMPTION

AUTHOR'S RENDITION

4. This FINANCING STATEMENT covers the following collateral:

The above named Secured Party, employer # 000112222, a living Sovereign Soul, hereby secures the rights, interest and title in Birth Certificate # 12345678 as received by the State of ????? Dept. of Health and Welfare (Div. of Vital Statistics) and the pledge represented by same, including but not limited to, the pignus, hypotheca, hereditaments, res, the energy and all products derived therefrom, but not limited to the all capitalized name, [ENS LEGIS NAME IN ALL CAPITAL LETTERS]; or any derivative thereof, and all contracts, signatures and agreements predicated on the ens legis STRAWMAN described above as Debtor.

Reclaim Your Sovereignty

"My God shall supply all your need according to his riches in glory by Christ Jesus." — *Phillipians 4:19*

Reclaim Your Sovereignty

"And there was silence in heaven about the space of half an hour." — *Revelation 8:1*

Reclaim Your Sovereignty

Oil Beneath Our Feet: America's Energy Non-Crisis
http://tinyurl.com/yayy296

Untold History Of America: Let The Truth Be Told
http://tinyurl.com/y8hwvzr

New Beginning Study Course: Connect The Dots And See
http://tinyurl.com/yc4jkyd

Monitions of a Mountain Man: Manna, Money, & Me
http://tinyurl.com/ygtkak8

Maine Street Miracle: Saving Yourself And America
http://tinyurl.com/ybss3ss

Commercial Redemption: The Hidden Truth
http://tinyurl.com/yj4otn4

Epistle to the Americans I: What you don't know about The Income Tax
http://tinyurl.com/yfplutf

Epistle to the Americans II: What you don't know about American History
http://tinyurl.com/yzme458

Epistle to the Americans III: What you don't know about Money
http://tinyurl.com/yzuffbe

CPSIA information can be obtained
at www.ICGtesting.com
Printed in the USA
LVHW051557030321
680485LV00012B/1738